PROGRAMMING FOR THE MASSES

gary a. mattison

Pearson
Custom
Publishing

Printed in the United States of America

10 9 8 7 6 5 4 3 2 1

Please visit our web site at www.pearsoncustom.com

ISBN 0–536–60313–8

BA 990708

PEARSON CUSTOM PUBLISHING
160 Gould Street/Needham Heights, MA 02494
A Pearson Education Company

DEDICATION

This text is dedicated to you, our student.

Best wishes and continued success.

May you fulfill all your academic dreams.

PREFACE

Purpose of This Text

This text will provide you an introduction to programming using a proven series of steps that are designed specifically for a person with no prior experience in programming. It emphasizes a working knowledge of logic and flowcharting as precursors to programming. With practice, practice, and more practice—and a feel for problem solving—you too can become a good programmer.

My objectives in writing this text were:

1. To produce a concise text that students will find easy to read and comprehend.

2. To teach good logic, problem solving, flowcharting, and programming skills.

3. To develop focused chapters by concentrating on important subjects, covering them succinctly but thoroughly.

4. To use realistic examples and exercises with which students can relate, appreciate, and feel comfortable.

5. To present the material in such a manner that, upon completion of this course, you will be confident enough in your abilities that you can reliably produce programs that will solve elementary business problems.

Unique and Distinguishing Features

Prerequisite Preparation. This course should be taken after you have completed an introductory computer information systems course.

From Simple to Complex. Topics are used in simple situations before being applied to complex problems. In this way, you get to know the construct before you use it in combination with previous constructs.

Continuous Examples. Beginning with the first topic, one primary example will be used whenever possible, throughout the text. The example will be modified in every chapter by the new constructs introduced in that chapter. This will provide you a continuity of thought that builds on the previous material. Understanding how the example problem was modified will help you complete the exercise set at the end of the section.

Exercises. All sections in this text, except for the "Introduction" section, have an exercise set that was carefully selected to focus on points that are essential to understanding the material in that chapter. You should attempt to do all the exercises and study their solutions.

Visual Basic 6.0 Included. THIS IS NOT A VISUAL BASIC COURSE! Even though a Working Model Edition of Visual Basic 6.0 is packaged with every copy of this text, its inclusion is solely to illustrate structured programming rules and constructs using a modern programming language. You will find that the enclosed limited edition of Visual Basic will be more than adequate for the purposes of this course.

ACKNOWLEDGMENTS

Many people are involved in the successful publication of this text. I wish to thank the people at Prentice Hall and Pearson Custom Publishing whose enthusiastic support made this book possible. Rick Spencer came up with the idea of a custom programming text to meet our needs over a year before the project became a reality. Once the decision was made, John O'Brien made sure the publication schedule was met. Over 30 percent of the text and examples in this text were taken directly from David I. Schneider's text, *An Introduction to Programming Using Visual Basic 6.0*. I thank him greatly for allowing me to use his material as the starting point for this text.

Thank you also to my fellow Strayer University professors who took the time to review this text and the logic upon which it is based. They are: Dr. James Cox, Dean Robert Goddard, Dean John Schuford, and Dean Donald Toddaro.

I need to extend a "Thank You" to our dedicated CIS group, the co-chairs of which are Dr. John Tucker and Prof. Terry Clapp, and our Grand Mentor, Dean Robert Gustavus. Members have been very supportive of my efforts from the beginning, and I thank them for that support. Members of the group are: Deans Wendy Abu-Rabi, Robert Goddard, John V. Murnane, and Farzan Soroushi, with an occasional visit from Jim Anderson, Thomas W. Pigg, and Michael Otaigbe; and Professors Irene Bruno, Joseph Chapman, David T. Lipp, Elsayed Mansour, Bryant L. Payden, George B. Reese, and Gerry Waldrop.

I would also like to thank my wife Kathy who has been very supportive of my efforts throughout the creation of this text and of my pursuit of my Ph.D. from Capella University.

Last but certainly not least, I am grateful to the Microsoft Corporation for its commitment to producing outstanding programming languages, and for its permission to include a copy of the Working Model Edition of Visual Basic 6.0 with each book.

CONTENTS

CHAPTER 1

BASIC PROBLEM SOLVING

1-1. Introduction

This is a book about problem solving with computers.

You accomplish all levels of problem solving in your every day life, from what to wear and what to eat, to selecting a life partner and which profession to pursue. Most of the time, you are unaware that you were using traditional decision-making methodologies. Within seconds, you identified the problem, generated alternative solutions, chose the best solution, decided which steps to take, placed those steps in a logical order, then put your plan into action, often without thinking much about the process itself. You have been doing that all your life.

However, you have not been using a computer to solve business problems all your life, so please do not expect to arrive at a neatly packaged solution in seconds. Nearly everyone can become a good—or even great—programmer. However, programming is like deciding what to wear to a formal event—it takes time and patience, and sometimes a lot of trial-and-error.

Understanding concepts, logic, and problem solving methodology are much more important to becoming a successful programmer than learning a specific language. If your logic is sound, the program will eventually work, and it will solve the problem. If your logic is defective, your program may or may not work, but it will never solve the problem. Therefore, this text begins with the foundation of all great programs . . . problem solving skills, sound logic, and conceptual thinking.

1-2. Problem Solving Concepts and Procedures

Problem solving means using a structured approach to generating feasible solutions to an abnormal situation. It is as much a state of mind as it is a fact of life. If you sincerely believe that you can find a solution to a situation, you will. Then, as you solve more and more problems, you will begin to find similarities in the methodologies and in the solutions themselves. Problem solving will be easier, faster, and you will accomplish it with more reliability, especially through practice.

The following **problem solving procedures** are the steps that must be taken for successful problem solving in a business environment. They are very much like solving problems with the computer. These steps are:

1. *Define the problem.* Determine what needs to be accomplished, then break the problem into its component parts. In this text, as in most texts, the problem and its requisite parts have been given to you. Gather facts about the parts that will help you understand the problem: how the parts relate to one another, and any limitations to which you must adhere (see *knowledge database* below).

3

2. *Generate alternatives.* The traditional methodology is brainstorming, or having a group come up with unqualified alternatives. Since you will normally accomplish this task alone, it is important to understand that there may be many correct ways to solve a problem. Attempt to generate at least two detailed alternatives.

3. *Evaluate the alternatives.* List the pros and cons of each alternative, according to the criteria (facts and final results) you determined when doing Step 1.

4. *Select the best alternative.* Choose the one that makes the most sense to you. By now, you should have a good idea of what is expected, and how to accomplish the solution.

5. *Implement the solution.* Execute the selected alternative, step-by-step, as planned. Be sure that your solution operates according to the limitations you discovered in Step 1.

6. *Evaluate the solution.* Check the outcome. First, is it a reasonable answer to the problem? Secondly, does it answer the problem fully and accurately?

In accomplishing problem solving, you make certain assumptions about what the person already knows about the situation. An important part of step 1, a **knowledge database** contains facts that must be known by the user prior to creating or implementing the solution. For instance, before you can detail the steps necessary to "*Peel a carrot*," you must assume that the person executing the task knows: (1) what a carrot is; (2) where to get the carrot from; (3) what a carrot peeler is; (4) where the carrot peeler is stored; (5) what a paring knife is; and (6) where the paring knife is stored. Then, beginning with "1–GET PARING KNIFE," you can detail the steps for your solution.

Using the six steps, the solution to "*Peel a carrot*" would look like this:

1. *Define the problem.* To peel a carrot, you must cut off its top, cut off a portion of its bottom, and peel off all of its skin. The carrot and all utensils required are given. *Knowledge database:* The user must know what a carrot is, which end is the top, what a carrot peeler is, how to use it properly, what a paring knife is, and how to use it properly.

2. *Generate alternatives.* Cut off the top and bottom of the carrot with a paring knife. Peel the carrot with the carrot peeler, or peel the carrot with the paring knife. (Note that both solutions have the first two steps in common, which may also occur in your problem solutions several times.)

3. *Evaluate the alternatives.* Using a paring knife to peel a carrot would be more dangerous and probably slower than using the carrot peeler.

4. *Select the best alternative.* The paring knife will be used to cut off the top and bottom of the carrot, and the carrot peeler will be used to peel the carrot.

5. *Implement the solution.*

    1. Get paring knife.
    2. Point blade away from you.
    3. Get carrot.
    4. Grip the carrot firmly in the middle.
    5. Place the carrot on a cutting surface.

6. Cut through the carrot approximately ¼" below the top of the carrot.

7. Rotate the carrot 180 degrees.

8. Cut through the carrot approximately 1" from the bottom.

9. Lift carrot from the cutting surface.

10. Get carrot peeler.

11. Hold carrot firmly at the top.

12. Position carrot peeler in the middle of the carrot.

13. Be sure that the peeler blades are in contact with the carrot.

14. Using a steady downward stroke, push the carrot peeler away from your body and past the end of the carrot.

15. Return the carrot peeler to its original starting position.

16. Rotate the carrot until the blades of the peeler are next to the section that was just peeled, but over a section that needs to be peeled.

17. Repeat steps 11 through 16 until the bottom half of the carrot has been peeled.

18. Hold carrot firmly at the bottom.

19. Position carrot peeler in the middle of the carrot, just above the unpeeled section at the top of the carrot.

20. Be sure that the peeler blades are in contact with the carrot.

21. Using a steady downward stroke, push the carrot peeler away from your body and past the end of the carrot.

22. Return the carrot peeler to its original starting position.

23. Rotate the carrot until the blades of the peeler are next to the section that was just peeled, but over a section that needs to be peeled.

24. Repeat steps 18 through 23 until the top half of the carrot has been peeled.

25. Inspect the carrot for any spots that were missed on the first try.

26. If the spot is on the bottom half, do steps 11 through 16 to remove the spot.

27. Repeat steps 25 and 26 until all the bottom half has been peeled.

28. If the spot is on the upper half, do steps 18 through 23 to remove the spot.

29. Repeat steps 25 and 28 until all the top half has been peeled.

30. Task completed.

6. ***Evaluate the solution.*** If the carrot is completely peeled, and it has no top stalk nor the very bottom section, the task is complete. Otherwise, begin at step 18 and check the carrot's surface again.

You probably had no idea that you went through *at least 30 steps* to peel one single carrot! However, this is an example of the level of detail that most program plans must contain. Note too that actions were not combined. Each step contained a singular action or command. That fact is extremely important. Combining too many actions in one command can prove problematic when trying to remove those inevitable planning and programming errors.

Exercise 1-2

You just built a robot, and you named this mechanical marvel "Manny." As you answer this set of questions, think of the answers in terms of telling Manny what to do. Manny "knows" only those facts that you place in its knowledge database and nothing else. Your solution is based on those facts, and must be sufficiently detailed so it leaves no process unfinished.

Determine the *knowledge database* first, and then use the *six problem-solving steps* to develop a solution to each of the following scenarios. Be sure to give your answers according to the six steps.

1. How to start a car.

2. How to scramble eggs.

3. How to find a book in a library.

4. How to get a glass of water.

5. State the methodology you would use to determine the largest number of any three numbers. Be specific. You cannot use, "Because I just know which is larger."

1-3. Logic and Logical Thinking

Logic deals with the principles of reasoning. Two people will seldom think exactly alike, although their basic flow of logic may be very similar. We use logic to draw specific conclusions from general facts, or make general inferences based on specific facts.

When associated with computer programming, **logic** *refers to the relationship between the elements of a program*. At first, this is a macro-perspective of input, processing, storage, and output, then later a detailed account of the interaction between commands and subroutines.

Logical thinking derives its roots from earlier known statements or events. For instance, it is logical to expect rain in April, or it is logical to assume that you will feel pain if you touch hot coals. You could have either heard these "truths," read them somewhere, or experienced them for yourself.

You used your own reasoning to successfully solve the problems in Section 1-2. It did not matter whether your solution matched that of the text or a classmate's; you had your own unique answers. Merely by completing the exercises, you added to your personal 'database' of experience and expertise. These experiences, the methods you used, and your ability to reason logically will help you establish the proper order of, and relationship between, the elements of your program.

"Normal logic" indicates a general consensus among a group or population about an idea, a process, or a thing. Many people fear the fact that their logic may be very different than that of others. As the saying goes, "You have nothing to fear but fear itself."

The fact that not everyone thinks alike is the key to finding a variety of acceptable solutions to a problem. For instance, there are many ways to build a bridge across a river, and each of them provides a successful solution to the problem. Different bridges may be better than the rest at different times, depending on the criteria used. However, the base fact is . . . they all work!

Individual logic is much the same. There is often a number of acceptable ways to design, develop, implement, or test something. On those few occasions that something does not work, learn from the mistake and move on. With so many paths to success, the best policy is to just . . . *trust your logic!*

Exercise 1-3

You have been patiently "training" Manny to do simple tasks. Right now, Manny "knows" only two commands:

STEP—This means he will take one step forward and stop.

TURN—This means he will turn 90° to the right and stop.

You need to give Manny (**M**) the proper series of commands (STEP or TURN) to get him through the following maze. Remember that he understands only the two commands, and you can give them to him only one command at a time. The numbers of steps for each hallway are inside the hall.

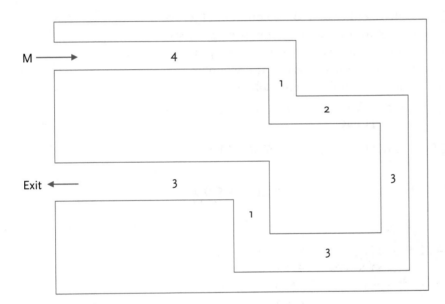

1. How many commands must be issued to Manny? What are they?
2. If Manny "learns" that a number after the command means to do the command that many times (i.e. STEP2 means take two steps and stop, and TURN2 means turn twice to the right and stop), what are the fewest commands you can give Manny to get it through the maze? What are they?

1-4. Conceptual Thinking

A concept is a general idea (or thought) that is generated from the mind. It is sometimes referred to as "the big picture" or "one over the world." As all-encompassing as it may seem, the creation of a concept is often rooted in the combination of past instances or occurrences with new or seemingly unrelated ideas, sometimes in unique and exciting ways.

In today's society, **concept** can also mean a plan or a scheme for getting something done. In this text, you will be doing both, connecting experience and thoughts, and developing plans. At first, you will be generating a plan to solve a problem, then as the problems get more complex, your problem analysis will be easier if you "see the big picture" first; that is, if you develop an appreciation for the nature and purpose of the problem before you attempt to detail the steps to solve it.

Therefore, **conceptual thinking** refers to drawing conclusions, formulating solutions, or interpreting a problem based on your past experiences with similar subject matter (your experiential database). The more you practice and gain experience with these processes, the better they will serve you when you are asked to conceive a plan, solve a problem, or just offer your opinion of something.

The exercises that follow will give you practice in logic and conceptual thinking. Although they may call for a bit of creativity, their purpose is two-fold: to let you draw on your experiential database, and to exercise and expand your ability to associate similar concepts.

Exercise 1-4

The pictographs in Exercises 1 through 12 either describe a common object or represent a well-known American saying. To solve them, think of items or sayings you have seen or heard on previous occasions; in other words, use your personal experience data base to help you answer these puzzlers. You will note after a few exercises that some of the solutions use similar methodologies.

Solve these pictographs. For example, **WEAR** would be *long underwear*.

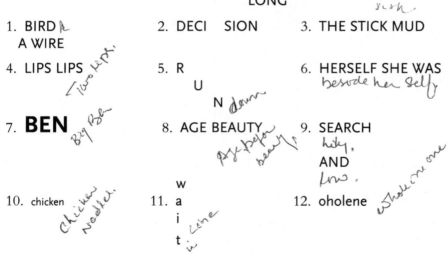

LONG

1. BIRD A
   A WIRE

2. DECI   SION

3. THE STICK MUD

4. LIPS LIPS

5. R
     U
        N

6. HERSELF SHE WAS

7. **BEN**

8. AGE BEAUTY

9. SEARCH
   AND

10. chicken

11. a
    i
    t
    w

12. oholene

For the following exercises, the numbers and letters provide a clue to the problem solution. Therefore, your previous numbers-based experience database will help. As an example, "26 L of the A" would be "26 Letters of the Alphabet".

13. 7 W of the W

14. 8 S on a S S

15. 9 P in the S S

16. 12 S of the Z

17. 13 S on the A F

18. 18 H on a G C

19. 32 D at which W F

20. 54 C in a D (with 2 J)

21. 88 P K

22. 90 D in a R A

23. 200 D for PG in M

24. 1001 A N

CHAPTER 2

PROBLEM SOLVING TOOLS

2-1. Introduction

Computers are excellent tools because they can do the same things reliably, over and over and at great speed. To insure that processing is done properly, you need to know the definition of operators, constants, and variables, for these items control how data is represented and how it is processed. You also need to know when to use them and what effect they have when accomplishing your processing tasks.

If you have taken a course in Algebra, you used constants and variables in solving equations. If you missed the joy of taking Algebra, all is not lost. This section helps you learn what constants and variables are, how they are used in data processing, then provides you practice problems in using both concepts. Constants, variables, and operators are the keys to successful problem solving. They help you produce software that is flexible enough to meet the needs of a dynamic business environment.

Operators tell the computer what type of processing to accomplish. Operators are an essential part of calculating data, making comparisons, and combining operations. The three main types of operators are mathematical operators, relational operators, and logical operators, and they are also presented in this chapter.

2-2. Numbers and Strings; Constants and Variables

Some of the most important aspects of computing pertain to mathematical calculations. "Number crunching" is one of the tasks for which computers are well suited.

However, the computer is very particular about what does and does not represent a numerical value. A number can exist in only one of two ways, either as a numeric constant or as a numeric variable.

A **numeric constant** is commonly known as a **number.** The value of a number will never change. 23 has always meant 2 tens and 3 ones, and will always mean that in our number system. Computer numbers are a bit more finicky than normal numbers. A computer number can contain three—and only three—things: a sign (+ or −), numbers (0 to 9 in any combination), and a decimal point. Commas, dollar signs, percent signs, dashes (as used in Social Security Account Numbers), and mixed numbers are *not* allowed. For example:

Invalid numbers:	23,000	$94.25	75%	893-15-2244	8 3/4
Valid numbers:	23000	94.25	0.75	893152244	8.75

A **numeric variable,** on the other hand, represents any number. It is a placeholder for the number until its value has been determined. In early math courses, you learned that the distance traveled is equal to the rate of travel times the total time traveling. Using the algebraic formula, you have:

11

d =rt

However, these letters are a bit cryptic, especially if you did not know that we were calculating distance. Therefore, from this point on, we will refer to quantities by giving them names. These names are commonly known as **meaningful variables.** Now the distance problem looks like this:

distance = rate x time

With meaningful variables, it is easy to see what we are trying to determine (distance), what data is needed (rate and time), and how that data must be processed (multiply rate times the time).

Since the equation uses variables instead of constants, we can use it to determine the variable *distance* whether driving 25 mph for 30 minutes, 40 mph for 15 minutes, or 55 mph for 2 hours. All we have to do is substitute the speed constant (i.e. 25) for the variable *speed,* and the time constant in hours (i.e. 0.5) for the variable *time,* then multiply the two.

distance = 25 x 0.5 = 12.5 (miles)

A **string** is a group of non-calculating characters. Many programmers refer to strings as *alphanumeric* data, or data that may contain alpha (letters or special characters), numeric (numbers), or both types of data. The most important aspect to remember about all strings is that *a string cannot be used in mathematical calculations.*

For instance, what is the value of your name times 2 plus 3? There is no answer to that question because your name has no numeric value. Another example would be to try to determine the value of your phone number divided by 5. You may be able to get an answer, but what would it represent? Not much.

Just as there were *numeric constants* and *numeric variables,* there *are string constants* and *string variables.* A **string constant** is a set of characters (including spaces) that will not change. The names of people and things, phrases and sentences, addresses, phone numbers, zip codes, Social Security Account Numbers, and so on are examples of string constants: non-calculating alphanumeric data.

String constants are noted by placing them in parenthesis. This is very important, for without the parenthesis, it is easy to mistake a string constant for a numeric variable. "BILL" the person (string constant) is much different than BILL (numeric variable) which is the amount you owe after purchasing something.

A **string variable** is a word that represents a string, much the same way a numeric variable represents a number. For instance, the string variable *Name* can be used to represent "ANN", "BILL", "Prentice-Hail, Inc.", or "Maple Avenue."

It could be difficult to tell the difference between a numeric variable and a string variable. Which is an appropriate response for the variable *Age,* the numeric constant 24, or the string constant "twenty-four years"? Both? Not really, for they are very different in nature. Only the numeric constant 24 can be used in a calculation.

To prevent confusion, a *standard naming convention* is used. A **standard naming convention** is a consistent methodology for identifying the type of variable being used. In this text, *num* will be placed in front of numeric variables, and *str* will be placed in front of string variables.

The correct response to *numAge* is 24, and the correct response to *strAge* is "twenty-four years." "24" would also be appropriate for *strAge* if you only want to display the age and not use it in a calculation. In general, the proper response to a numeric variable is a numeric constant, and the proper response to a string variable is a string constant.

The equality sign (=) is used to *assign a value* to a variable, which may be a constant or an expression consisting of other variables. If you think of the equal sign as an arrow pointing to the left, it may help remind you that the value of the right side is being assigned to the variable on the left. Finally, a plus sign (+) between two strings concatenates, or joins, them, i.e. "Can" + "not" = "Cannot."

■ Exercise 2-2

For each of the following, determine (1) whether it is valid or invalid, then (2) whether it is (or was supposed to be) a numeric constant, numeric variable, string constant, or string variable.

ITEM	VALID OR INVALID?	TYPE OF ITEM
1). 23,000.00	invalid	Numeric Const
2). "$23,000.00"	valid	String Numeric
3). Age	Invalid	Numeric variable
4). 0.3164789	valid	Numeric Const Variable
5). strStreetNum	valid	String variable Num Const
6). 7.4%	invalid	numeric const
7). numPayRate	invalid	Num variable
8). num66	valid	num Const variable
9). 804-237-7721	invalid	Num variable
10). Street name	invalid	String const variable

Give the value of the variable for each of the following.

11). numTotal = 256 + 24

$256 + 24 = 280$

12). numSale = numPrice − 2.00, when numPrice is 79.95

$79.95 − 2 = 77.95$

13). numTotal = numSales1 + numSales2, when numSales1 is 3100 numSales2 is 1600

$3100 + 1600 = 4700$

14). strName = strInit + strName, when strInit = "G.", strName = "Addams"

"G. Addams"

15). strAddr = strNum + strName, when strName = "Luck St.", strNum = "13"

"13 Luck St."

2-3. Mathematical Operators

By now you are aware that computers have their own language. The following illustrates the process, the original expression and symbol, and its corresponding computer expression and symbol.

Process	Arithmetic Expression	Computer Expression
Add	$2 + 3$	$2 + 3$
Subtract	$2 - 3$	$2 - 3$
Multiply	2×3	$2 * 3$
Divide	$2 \div 3$	$2 / 3$
Exponent	2^3	$2 \wedge 3$

Calculations using exponents are actually easy, even if you have never used exponents before now. When you see an exponential expression like $2 \wedge 3$, it means to take the first number, 2, write it down 3 times, then multiply. For instance, $2 \wedge 3$ becomes $2 * 2 * 2$, which means $2 * 2 = 4$, and $4 * 2 = 8$. Another way to manually calculate these numbers is:

$$2 \wedge 3 \text{ which becomes } 2 * 2 * 2 = 8$$

$$4$$

$$8$$

Algebraic expressions in their original form are also invalid for computer calculations. They need to be converted into single line expressions, as in the exponent example above. Other examples are:

$5a$ in algebra becomes $5 * a$

$3y^2$ in algebra becomes $3 * y \wedge 2$

$\dfrac{x + y}{z}$ in algebra becomes $(x + y) / z$

$3(x - z^2)$ in algebra becomes $3 * (x - z \wedge 2)$

The computer uses mathematical symbols in single line format to rapidly calculate numbers with remarkable precision. A very strict hierarchy of processing is used to control processing and maintain this accuracy.

The **Hierarchy of Mathematical Operations** defines the order in which all mathematical processing is accomplished. If the expression does not contain an operation of that level (i.e. no parenthesis), then the computer will skip to the next level (exponents) and continue processing. This procedure will continue until all mathematical operations have been completed.

A handy acronym for remembering the hierarchy is *PEMDAS,* formed by using the first letter of each mathematical operation. The saying that is used with equal frequency is, *Please Excuse My Dear Aunt Sally.* Once again, the saying is formed by using the first letter of each operation to create the saying.

Level 1	( )	**Parenthesis**—Anything in parenthesis is done first. If there are multiple parenthesis, the inside most set is calculated first, then processing works outward until all parenthesis are completed.
Level 2	∧	**Exponent**—All exponential expressions are calculated starting with any exponent in a parenthesis, then continuing with the expression on the left.
Level 3	∗ /	**Multiply** or **Divide**—Both of these operations are on the same level, and are equal in precedence. Therefore, either multiply or divide will be executed depending on which operation is first from the left. Continue until all operations at this level are completed.
Level 4	+ −	**Add** or **Subtract**—Both of these operations are on the same level, and both are equal in precedence. Therefore, either add or divide will be executed depending on which operation is first from the left. Continue until there are no more operations to be completed.

Figure 2-1. Hierarchy of Mathematical Operations

The following examples illustrate how the computer (and you) will use PEMDAS to properly calculate an expression. Shown are two techniques for employing PEMDAS.

$$3 + 4 \wedge 3 - 2 =$$
$$3 + 64 - 2 =$$
$$67 \quad - 2 = 65$$

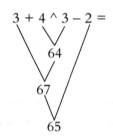

$$3 + 4 \wedge 3 - 2 =$$

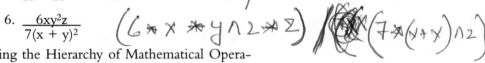

Exercise 2-3

Convert the following from algebraic expressions to computer expressions.

1. $3b$ 3 ∗ b

2. $3x + 4y^2$ (3 ∗ x) + (4 ∗ y ∧ 2)

3. $\dfrac{x}{2}$ x / 2

4. $\dfrac{2a + 2b}{2a - 2b}$ (2 ∗ a + 2 ∗ b) / (2 ∗ a − 2 ∗ b)

5. $4(ax + b)^2$ 4 ∗ (a ∗ x + b) ∧ 2

6. $\dfrac{6xy^2z}{7(x + y)^2}$ (6 ∗ x ∗ y ∧ 2 ∗ z) / (7 ∗ (y + x) ∧ 2)

Solve the following exercises using the Hierarchy of Mathematical Operations. *Hint:* calculate all expressions at one level before moving to the next level.

7. $1 + 3 ∗ 4$

8. $7 \wedge 2$

9. $2 \wedge 5 / 4 ∗ 2$

10. $3 / ((4 + 5) - 6)$

11. $(5 - 3) ∗ 4 - 2$

12. $3 ∗ ((-2) \wedge 5) + 6 / 2$

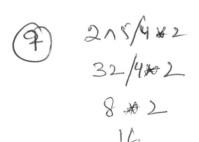

Evaluate the numeric expression where a = 2, b = 3, and c = 4.

13. (a * b) + c   14. a * (b + c)

15. (1 + b) * c   16. a ^ c

17. b ^ (c − a)   18. (c − a) ^ b

19. a ^ (a + b)   20. c ^ b ^ a

2-4. Relational and Logical Operators

A **relational operator** is used to compare a number to a number, or to compare a string to a string. Figure 2-2 shows relational operators and their meanings.

Mathematical Notation	Computer Notation	Numeric Meaning	String Meaning
=	=	equal to	identical to
≠	< >	not equal to	different from
<	<	less than	precedes alphabetically
>	>	greater than	follows alphabetically
≤	<=	less than or equal to	precedes alphabetically or is identical to
≥	>=	greater than or equal to	follows alphabetically or is identical to

Figure 2-2. Relational operators

For example, logical operators would be used to determine whether one number is larger than another, i.e. is 7 less than 5 (or 7 < 5), or whether one string follows another, i.e. does "cat" follow "cart" alphabetically (or "cat" > "cart"). When sets of numbers or strings involve logical operators, they create conditions.

A **condition** is an expression involving relational operators that will ultimately be used to make a decision. Conditions are evaluated as being either *True* or *False*. In the examples above, the condition 7 < 5 evaluates False, for 7 is not less than 5. The condition "cat" > "cart" evaluates True, for "cat" will follow "cart" when they are put in alphabetical order. Two strings are compared working from left to right, character by character, to determine which should precede the other.

Here are a few pointers that deal with the order of numbers and strings.

1. Uppercase letters precede lowercase letters in the ASCII (American Standard for Information Interchange) table. Therefore, "Dog" would come before "cat" simply because of the uppercase "D." "Dog" would also precede "dog" for the same reason.

2. Numbers used in a string, i.e. "9east", precede uppercase letters. Therefore, "9east" < "Avenue" evaluates True.

3. Use a number line if you have trouble with negative numbers. Does the condition −5 > −10 evaluate True or False? A quick check on the number line shows that −5 is greater than −10 since it is farther to the right than -10.

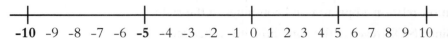

4. Conditions can also contain numeric or string variables. However, they can only be evaluated when a constant is finally substituted for the variable. numA > numB is a valid conditon, but numeric constants must be substituted for A and B to determine whether the condition is True or False.

5. While it is possible to compare numbers to strings using their ASCII value, it is not practical decision-making. It is very much like the old adage, "Comparing apples to oranges."

Programming situations often require more complex conditions than a mere comparison of two numbers or two strings. **Logical operators** allow us to combine and/or compare conditions for complex decision making. The following chart gives the three logical operators and their effect on the evaluation of the expression:

Logical Operator	Effect	To Evaluate As True . . .
AND	Combines two conditions	Both conditions must be true.
OR	Compares two conditions	Only one condition has to be true.
NOT	Reverses the state of the condition. For example, = becomes < >, < becomes > =, > becomes < =, and vice versa for each set.	The condition must be false.

Figure 2-3. Logical operators

To state that the value of a numeric variable, n, is between 2 and 5, the proper condition is:

$$(2 < n) \text{ AND } (n < 5)$$

Only two whole numbers qualify as valid answers. Remember that both conditions, $(2 < n)$ and $(n < 5)$, must be true to have the complex condition evaluate as True. Therefore, the answer is either $n = 3$ or $n = 4$. What about 2? What about 5? No, neither one will work. Any value other than 3 or 4 would result in an evaluation of False.

The use of parenthesis with logical operators will often improve readability. However, they are not always present. You may want to insert your own parenthesis, especially when complex conditions include multiple logical operators, algebraic expressions, and/or constants.

Finally, there is a strict hierarchy among the different operators that goes from level 1 to 3, including internal priorities within each level.

1. *Mathematical Operators.* **Arithmetic operations are carried out according to the Hierarchy of Mathematical Operations.**

2. *Relational Operators.* **All relational operators are equal, so processing begins with the leftmost relational operator and continues to the right.**

3. *Logical Operators.* **Since NOT reverses the condition, it is processed first. AND is next because it requires that both sets be True. OR is last since it only requires that one set be True.**

Exercise 2-4

Assume that $a = 2$ and $b = 3$. Determine whether each of the following is either True or False.

1. $3 * a = 2 * b$ 2. $(5 - a) * b < 7$

3. $b <= 3$ 4. $a ^\wedge b = b ^\wedge a$

5. $a ^\wedge (5 - 2) > 7$ 6. $(a < b)$ OR $(b < a)$

7. $(a * a < b)$ OR NOT $(a * a < a)$

8. $((a = b)$ AND $(a * a < b * b))$ OR $((b < a)$ AND $(2 * a < b))$

Determine whether the condition evaluates as True or False.

9. "9W" < > "9w"   10. "Inspector" < "gadget"

11. "Car" < "Train"   12. "99" > "ninety-nine"

13. ("Duck" < "pig") AND ("pig" < "big")

14. $(7 < 34)$ AND ("7" > "34")

Suppose the numeric variable *n* has a value of 4 and the string variable *ans* has a value of "Y". Determine whether each of the following conditions evaluates as True or False.

15. $(2 < n)$ AND $(n < 6)$ 16. $(2 < n)$ OR $(n = 6)$

17. NOT $(n < 6)$ 18. $(ans = "Y")$ OR $(ans = "y")$

19. $(ans = "Y")$ AND $(ans = "y")$

20. $((2 < n)$ AND $(n = 5 + 1))$ OR $(ans = "No")$

CHAPTER 3

PROGRAMMING CONCEPTS

3-1.   Introduction

The basic concept of programming is finding a computer-based solution to a business problem. This can only be accomplished through good programming, and successful programming requires planning.

A recipe provides a good example of a plan. The ingredients and the amounts are determined by what is to be baked. That is, the *output* determines the *input* and the *processing*. The recipe, or plan, reduces the number of mistakes you might make if you tried to bake with no plan at all.

Although it is difficult to imagine a construction company building a bridge or a factory without an architect's detailed plan, many programmers (particularly students in their first programming course) frequently try to write programs without first making a careful plan.

The more complicated the problem, the more complex the plan must be. You will spend much less time working on a program if you devise a carefully thought out step-by-step plan and test it before actually writing a program. Remember the programmer's saying, "Be slow to code." In terms of another pertinent saying, "Prior planning prevents poor performance."

Many programmers plan their programs using a sequence of steps referred to as the **program development cycle**. The steps in the program development cycle are very similar to the six steps you already used in Problem Solving Procedures in Chapter 1. You will find a distinct similarity between them.

The following step-by-step process will enable you to use your time efficiently and help you design error-free programs that produce the desired output.

1. *Analyze the problem.* Define the problem. Be sure you understand what the problem should do in terms of output, input, processing, and possibly storage. Have a clear idea of the relationship between these processes. The sequence of input, processing, storage and output is covered in the next section.

2. *Design the solution.* Plan the solution to the problem. Find a logical sequence of steps that solve the problem, and state those steps in terms of a *flowchart* or *pseudocode*. Every detail should appear in the flowchart or pseudocode, including obvious steps. These two methods will be explained in Section 3-3 of this chapter.

3. *Check the solution.* Use real data to *desk-check* the flowchart to insure that the logic and order of the steps are correct. Desk-checking is explained in Section 3-4 of this chapter.

4. *Choose the interface.* Select the Visual Basic objects that will accomplish the specific input, processing, and output inferred by your flowchart. The specific objects you will use will be presented in Chapter 4.

5. *Code the program.* Write the *source code* (program) according to the sequence and processes that you used in your flowchart. Source code and source code commands are covered in Chapters 5 through 9.

6. *Test and debug the program.* Testing is the process of identifying errors in a program, and debugging is the process of correcting those errors. You may find problems in your program that Visual Basic did not catch when you were entering the source code. Do not be discouraged. Relatively few programs are ever flawlessly written on the first attempt. Debugging programs is presented in detail in Section 4-4.

You will get to apply the first three steps of this procedure later in this chapter. The last three steps will be used in following chapters.

3-2.   How the Computer Processes Data

The use of a specific programming language is not important to the purposes of this text. All computers take in data, manipulate them, store the results either temporarily or permanently, and give the desired information. These processes are referred to as input, processing, storage, and output. These operations are graphically presented in Figure 3-1.

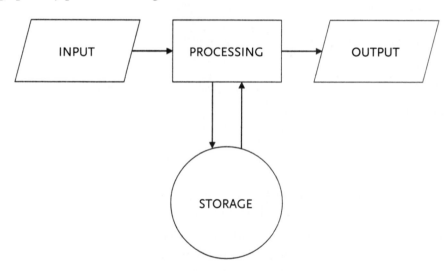

Figure 3-1. The four basic computer processes.

All programs are based on these four processes, although they may not contain all four. For instance, storage is seldom addressed in any of the earlier programs. Various programming languages have their own specific commands to accomplish these processes. Therefore, a key to good programming is to first know which processes are being addressed in the problem, determine the order in which they occur, and finally choose which programming command or commands will satisfy requirements.

As you read in the previous section, the first step in program planning is to *analyze the problem.* When you analyze the problem, you are trying to determine the data that needs to be input, processing that will take place, perhaps any storage required, and definitely what output is needed. To do this, you need to be able to divide the problem in term of processes. This normally begins by first identifying the output required, then all data to be input, and finally the processing required to turn the input into the requested output. Take a look at the following problem.

An employee's gross pay is calculated by multiplying the rate of pay times the number of hours worked.

I-P-O diagramming is a technique that will help you divide the problem into its important parts and see what is needed to accomplish the rest of the program planning steps. Place parenthesis ( ) around the passage that deals with *output*, brackets [ ] around *input*, and underline any *processing* required. After you had accomplished these steps, the example would appear as:

An employee's (gross pay) is calculated by underline{multiplying the} [rate of pay] underline{times the} [number of hours worked].

You learned in Section 3-1 that the *output* dictates what *input* is required and the *processing* the input must undergo. From the preceding example, you can easily see that (gross pay) requires that [rate of pay] and [number of hours worked] be entered by someone so your program can multiply rate of pay times number of hours worked.

DO NOT SELL THIS STEP SHORT!!! Being able to analyze a problem in terms of input, processing, and output is the key to being a successful programmer. The logic you use to analyze problems carries over into flowcharting, selecting objects for the user interface, and creating your program, all of which will help you solve the problem. *Take the time to do this step well!*

Next, we need to present this information in terms of a program plan. The program plan will become your "roadmap" for problem resolution. There are three primary design tools you may use to establish this roadmap: hierarchy charts, pseudocode, and flowcharts.

The **hierarchy chart** shows the overall program structure and how the program has been divided into subprograms called modules. Hierarchy charts are also called structure charts, HIPO (Hierarchy plus Input-Process-Output) charts, top-down charts, or VTOC (Visual Table Of Contents) charts.

Hierarchy charts depict the organization of a program but omit the specific processing logic. They describe what each part, or *module* does, and how the modules relate to each other. A **module** is a collection of related actions placed in their own sub-program. The details of how the modules work are omitted.

The chart is read from top to bottom and left to right. Each module may be subdivided into a succession of sub-modules that branch out under it. The hierarchy chart shown in Figure 3-2 represents the methodology for calculating gross pay.

The main benefit of hierarchy charts is in the initial planning of a complex program. We break down the major parts of a program so we can see what must be done in terms of input, processing, and output. This process is called the **divide-and-conquer method**. You separate the problem into its related parts, then put those parts in a subprogram all their own.

The Main Module controls the processing. Sub-modules are called into memory by the Main Module, and they signal the Main when they have completed their processing. This arrangement is a lot like the workplace. The boss (AKA Main Module) has specialists who possess specific skills to perform a set of tasks. The boss tells a worker what is to be done, and the worker does it. When the tasks have been completed, the worker takes the finished product to back to the boss, and the boss passes the task to the next expert for their added touch, and so on until the job has been completed.

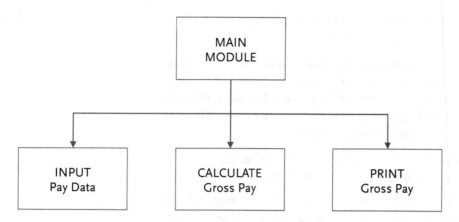

Figure 3-2. Hierarchy chart for the Gross Pay example.

Since the hierarchy chart is used primarily to solve complex problems, we will not use this tool until the later chapters. For now, one of the next two methods are preferred since they are geared for more straight-forward program planning.

Pseudocode is an English-like abbreviation of actual computer code (hence, *pseudo-code*). Pseudocode allows the programmer to focus on the steps required to solve a problem rather than on how to use the programming language. The programmer can even describe the solution in terms of commands and variables without being worried about language syntax.

Pseudocode has several advantages. It is compact and probably will not extend for many pages as do most flowcharts. The plan looks like the code to be entered in the computer, so it is preferred by many seasoned programmers. Finally, unlike hierarchy charts and flowcharts, pseudocode can be generated using a normal word processor. The document can then be copied directly into the programming language's work area and converted to source code. This saves a lot of time.

However, the proper use of pseudocode depends on the programmer having some knowledge of programming before using pseudocode for design work. Therefore, this text will use a tool that replaces the English-like statements with geometric symbols and very abbreviated statements. Flowcharting is the methodology most instructors prefer to have their first-time programmers use to outline the problem.

■ Exercise 3-2

For each of the following questions, develop the answer using the first step of the Problem Solving Procedures, *Analyze the Problem*, which is described in this section. Use the *I-P-O diagramming* technique for each exercise.

Remember to reduce all input, processing and output to its simplest form. Do not combine operations, i.e. two inputs, unless the situation calls for it.

1. Once a user has entered any two numbers, add the numbers together and display their sum.

2. After a person enters their first name and last name, print their entire name on one line.

3. Have a person enter their name and age, determine what a person's age would be ten years from now, then print their name and age in ten ears.

4. Find the number of square yards of carpet needed to cover a room that is 12 feet by 15 feet. (area = length * width, and 1 square yard = 9 square feet).

5. Calculate the total bill when a customer buys any three items from a menu. (Use this data for a test case: lemonade for 75 cents, a cheeseburger for $1.25, and french fries for 90 cents.) Then print out each item with its associated cost, and the total cost. Remember that you should allow this program to calculate any three items selected from the menu.

3-3. Flowcharting and Flowcharting Symbols

A **flowchart** is a visual means of representing both the processes and sequence of processes involved in solving the problem. It is a design tool that features both graphical and textual details. **Flowcharting symbols** are used to create flowcharts. Most symbols have one meaning, although there are a select few symbols that have two different meanings. The flowcharting symbols you will use, their corresponding purpose, and symbol usage rules are as follows:

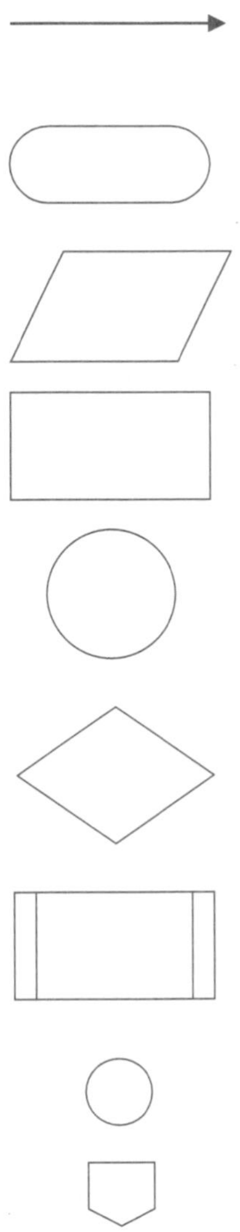

Flowline. This is used to connect flowcharting symbols. The arrowhead is used to indicate the direction of the data flow.

Start or Stop. Also called a terminal, this symbol is used at the beginning and at the end of every task, program, and subprogram. Start has only one flowline exiting it, and Stop has only one flowline entering it.

Input or Output. Data to be input is placed in the symbol that appears first, and data that will be output (displayed or printed) is placed in a symbol that will later occur. Input and Output symbols have only one flowline entering or exiting.

Processing. This symbol is used to indicate arithmetic and data manipulation operations. The data and operator are indicated inside the symbol. A processing block has only one entrance and one exit.

Storage. There are many different symbols for the many different types of storage. A large circle is a generic storage symbol that can mean temporary (RAM) or permanent (disk) storage. This symbol will be used very little in this text.

Decision. Used in conjunction with relational and/or logical operators to obtain an evaluation of True or False, Yes or No. It has one entrance and two exits. One exit is taken when the evaluation is True, and the other is taken when the evaluation is False.

Pre-determined process. Also called a Process Module, this symbol is used to indicate a block of processing tasks. These tasks are processed elsewhere in a program, in what you will soon be calling a subprogram or subprocedure.

On-page connector. Used to connect segments of a flowchart on the same page. Use A, B, C, etc.

Off-page connector. Used to connect segments of a flowchart on different pages. Use 1, 2, 3, etc.

Figure 3-3. Flowcharting symbols.

Flowcharts should "flow" from the top of the page to the bottom. Although the symbols used in flowcharts are standard, no standards exist for the amount of detail required within each symbol. Figure 3-4 is the flowchart for calculation of gross pay, the example previously used in this chapter.

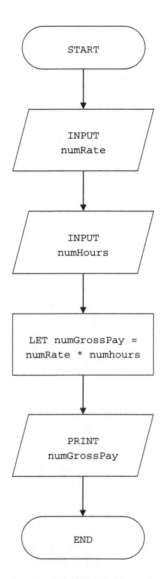

Figure 3-4. Flowchart for the Gross Pay example.

Exercise 3-3

For each of the following questions, develop the answer using *Design the Procedures,* the second step in the Problem Solving Procedures. A good place to start would be the I-P-O diagrams you did for these exercises in Exercise 3-2.

Design the solution with a complete flowchart using the proper symbols from this section. Remember to reduce all input, processing and output to its simplest form. Do not combine operations, i.e. two inputs, unless the situation calls for it.

1. Once a user has entered any two numbers, add the numbers together and display their sum.

2. After a person enters their first name and last name, print their entire name on one line.

3. Have a person enter their name and age, determine what a person's age would be ten years from now, then print their name and age in ten years.

4. Find the number of square yards of carpet needed to cover a room that is 12 feet by 15 feet. (area = length * width, and 1 square yard = 9 square feet).

5. Calculate the total bill when a customer buys any three items from a menu. (Use this data for a test case: lemonade for 75 cents, a cheeseburger for $1.25, and french fries for 90 cents.) Then print out each item with its associated cost, and the total cost. Remember that you should allow this program to calculate any three items selected from the menu.

3-4. Desk Checking Using Annotated Flowcharts

Soon, you will be able to produce reliable flowcharts that will require little if any adjustment from your original design. However, it is not uncommon for beginning programmers to experience less-than-perfect designs. Fortunately, there are techniques you can use to identify and rectify these design flaws.

Tracing is a technique used to "trace," or review quickly, the overall logic flow of the flowchart. Tracing will identify processes that were left out of the design, or ones that were placed out of order. However, tracing does not present the programmer a sufficient amount of detail. For that task, we use desk-checking.

Desk-checking is a technique of checking flowchart processes and the order of processing by substituting constants for the variables. Data used to check the flowchart should be standard and non-standard data. When that data is written on the flowchart itself, it is then known as an **annotated flowchart**. We will now convert the flowchart from the previous example into an annotated flowchart.

The main advantage of using a flowchart to plan a task is that it provides a pictorial representation of the task, which makes the logic easier to follow. We can clearly see every step and how each step is connected to the next. Converting the flowchart to an annotated flowchart increases your understanding of the task plan and simultaneously identifies potential errors.

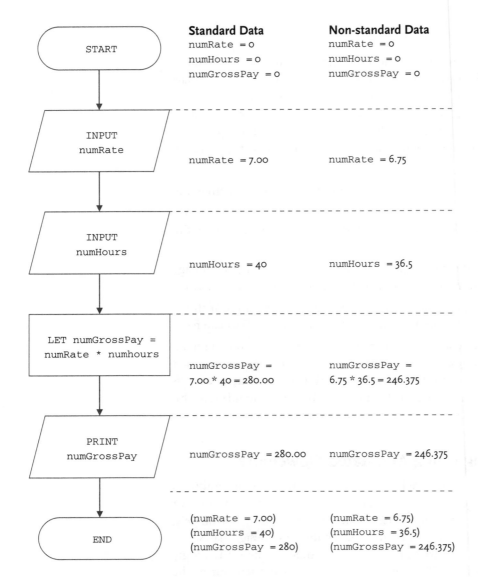

	Standard Data	Non-standard Data
START	numRate = 0 numHours = 0 numGrossPay = 0	numRate = 0 numHours = 0 numGrossPay = 0
INPUT numRate	numRate = 7.00	numRate = 6.75
INPUT numHours	numHours = 40	numHours = 36.5
LET numGrossPay = numRate * numhours	numGrossPay = 7.00 * 40 = 280.00	numGrossPay = 6.75 * 36.5 = 246.375
PRINT numGrossPay	numGrossPay = 280.00	numGrossPay = 246.375
END	(numRate = 7.00) (numHours = 40) (numGrossPay = 280)	(numRate = 6.75) (numHours = 36.5) (numGrossPay = 246.375)

Figure 3-5. Fully annotated flowchart.

The major disadvantage with flowcharts is that when a program is very large, the flowcharts may continue for many pages, making them difficult to follow and to modify. In this text, you will not encounter programs that require over two pages of flowcharting, given that you can fit two flowchart columns on one page. In most cases, programmers use a combination of hierarchy charts and pseudocode to design longer programs.

Exercise 3-4

For each of the following questions, develop the answer using the third step in the Problem Solving Procedures, *Check the Solution*. A good place to start would be the flowcharts you did in Exercise 3-3 for these same questions. Convert the original flowcharts to an annotated flowchart as described in this section.

1. Once a user has entered any two numbers, add the numbers together and display their sum.

2. After a person enters their first name and last name, print their entire name on one line.

3. Have a person enter their name and age, determine what a person's age would be ten years from now, then print their name and age in ten years.

4. Find the number of square yards of carpet needed to cover a room that is 12 feet by 15 feet. (area = length * width, and 1 square yard = 9 square feet).

5. Calculate the total bill when a customer buys any three items from a menu. (Use this data for a test case: lemonade for 75 cents, a cheeseburger for $1.25, and french fries for 90 cents.) Then print out each item with its associated cost, and the total cost. Remember that you should allow this program to calculate any three items selected from the menu.

CHAPTER 4

VISUAL BASIC: OBJECTS AND PROCEDURES

4-1.   Introduction

If you were to develop a standard Visual Basic application, two elements would be key in its design; the interface and event-driven programming. The **interface** is what the user sees, or in other words, the programmer's screen design. Event-driven programs are controlled by "events" initiated by the user, each of which has its own code, rather than sequential programs whose execution was pre-determined by the programmer.

However, as was mentioned in the beginning of this text, this is not a book about developing Visual Basic applications. Visual Basic is merely the language being used to demonstrate programming concepts and syntax rules while being mindful of the user interface.

Therefore, we will be employing Visual Basic a in more traditional role, that of a procedure-oriented language. The sequence of processes is all-important in procedural programming languages, so the order in which things occur will remain important. One aspect of Visual Basic that will be retained is the concept of objects used in the design of the interface. The four basic objects introduced next will be used throughout the rest of this book.

The transition from program requirements to the specific objects needed to fulfill those requirements is an important one. Using an incorrect object will change the nature of the processing and will probably change the output. Using the correct objects will help reinforce your logic and insure that the user gets the program they are anticipating.

In this chapter, we will begin to put these concepts together by first understanding which object is used when. Then you are introduced to the Visual Basic interface, and finally you will create each of these objects in a tutorial.

4-2.   Four Basic Objects

You will be using four Visual Basic objects initially to represent input, processing, output, and comments placed in the user interface. The key to selecting the correct object depends on the stated need: is it input, processing or output? The following table shows the requirements of the program design and the object that will fulfill that need. You will create these objects later in this section, so you will soon get to see what the objects look like.

Of the four objects, only the command button executes a program. The others are called upon as needed by the program contained in the command button. You will learn how to enter the code in the command button in the next chapter. For now, the emphasis is on selecting the correct object for the need.

Using the standard example of calculating gross pay, we need one picture box for the output, two text boxes for input (one each for *rate of pay* and *hours worked*), and a command button to process the program. Labels will be placed

PROCESS	OBJECT	PURPOSE
INPUT	**Text Box**	To obtain input prior to program execution.
PROCESS	**Command Button**	Contains the program code to execute the program.
OUTPUT	**Picture Box**	To display output.
- - - - - -	**Label**	To place a line of descriptive text next to a text box or a picture box.

Figure 4-1. Four initial design objects and their purpose

in front of the two text boxes identifying which one is for which input. A label will also be used to identify the nature of the output.

Now that the correct objects have been selected for the intended purposes, we will walk through the steps of creating these objects in Visual Basic. As an initial guideline, design the interface so the objects will appear in the order in which they occur: input, processing, and output. These can be arranged top to bottom or left to right, but they should be placed in the form in a logical order.

1. *Open the Visual Basic program.* (*Note:* You must have Visual Basic installed on your computer before continuing.) Click on "Start", "Programs", "Microsoft Visual Basic 6.0", and the "Microsoft Visual Basic 6.0" that will appear in the pop-up bar. You will see the *New Project window,* shown below. The New Project window is a part of all versions of Visual Basic 6.0, including the Working Model Edition that was enclosed with this text.

Figure 4-2. New Project window.

The main part of the window is tabbed with three tabs—"New", "Existing", and "Recent". You use the "New" tab to create a new Visual Basic project, and you would use the "Existing" tab to open a project that you have already created and saved. The "Recent" tab will not be used often since we will be either creating new projects or opening existing ones.

The number of icons showing will either be three (with the Working Model and Learning Editions) or thirteen (with the Professional and Enterprise Editions). We will use only the "New" tab and the "Standard.EXE" icon, so double-click on the "Standard.EXE" icon.

The initial Visual Basic screen appears as shown in Figure 4-3. The screen layout varies slightly with the different versions of Visual Basic. However, if you are missing parts of the screen, click on "View" in the menu bar and select the part(s) of the window you are missing from the pull-down menu. You may have to repeat this step several times until your screen contains all eight elements.

The **Menu Bar** of the Visual Basic screen is located directly under the title bar. It displays the commands you use to work with Visual Basic. Some of the menus, like "File", "Edit", "View", and "Window", are common to most Windows applications. Others, such as "Project", "Format", and "Debug", provide commands specific to programming in Visual Basic.

The **Toolbar,** located immediately under the menu bar, is a collection of icons that carry out standard operations when clicked. For example, the fifth icon, which looks like a diskette, can be used to save the current program to a disk. To reveal the function of a Toolbar icon, position the mouse pointer over the icon for a few seconds.

The **Toolbox** is a collection of objects (controls) that can be placed on the form. It is located on the left side of the initial screen. Each icon represents an object.

The large stippled **Form Window,** or **Form** for short, becomes a Windows window when a program is executed. Most information displayed by the project, including the objects that make up the design interface, appears on the form.

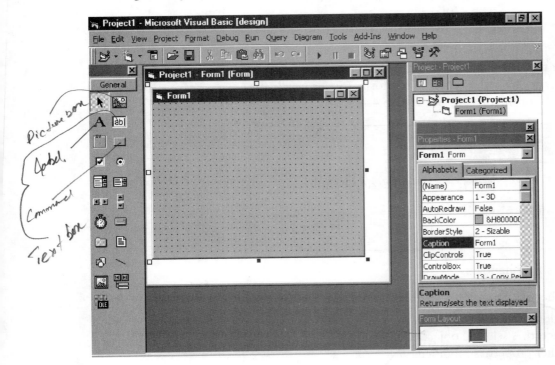

Figure 4-3. Initial Visual Basic screen.

The **Project Container window** is the white area that surrounds the form. It contains all the objects pertinent to that project. It can be resized according to interface requirements.

The **Project Explorer window,** located in the upper right portion of the screen, is a quick reference to the projects (and forms in the projects) that are on the source disk. This window will be seldom used, so close it.

The **Properties window** is used to change how objects look and react, and it is just below the project explorer window. We will use this window primarily to change the text in the objects.

The **Form Layout window** is the last window we cover, located in the bottom right portion of the screen. It allows you to position the location of the form when the program is executed using a small graphical representation of the screen. We will not be using this window in this text, so you can close it.

The four objects we will be selecting are represented by the following icons in the Toolbox:

 Text boxes—You use a text box primarily to get information, referred to as input, from the user.

 Command buttons—The user clicks a command button to initiate an action. They are the only object that contains programs for execution.

 Picture boxes—You use a picture box to display text or graphics output.

 Labels—You place a label to the left of a text box to tell the user what type of information to enter into the text box. You also use labels to identify output from picture boxes.

Objects are created in a design form in the Project Container window, and a toolbox is used to place the objects in the design form, all of which will be covered next. First, place a text box on the form to be used for input.

TEXT BOX Tutorial:

1. Double-click on the text box icon. A rectangle with eight small squares, called sizing handles, appears at the center of the form. (*Sizing handles* are used to change the size of the object.) See Figure 4-4.

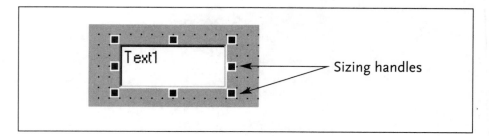

Figure 4-4. Text box with sizing handles.

2. Click anywhere on the form outside the rectangle to remove the handles.

3. Click on the rectangle to restore the handles. An object showing its handles is said to be **selected.** A selected object can have its size altered, location changed, and other properties modified.

4. Move the mouse arrow to the sizing handle in the center of the right side of the text box. The cursor should change to a double arrow. Hold down the left mouse button and move the mouse to the right. The text box is stretched to the right. Similarly, grabbing the text box by one of the other handles and moving the mouse stretches the text box in another direction. For instance, you use the handle in the upper-left corner to stretch the text box up and to the left simultaneously. Handles can also be used to make the text box smaller.

5. Move the mouse arrow to any point of the text box other than a handle, hold down the left mouse button, and move the mouse. You can now drag the text box to a new location. Using steps 4 and 5, you can place a text box of any size, or any other object of any size, anywhere on the form.

6. Press F4 to activate the Properties window. (You can also activate the Properties window by clicking on it or clicking on the Properties window icon on the Toolbar.) See Figure 4-5. The first line of the Properties window, also called the Object box, reads "Text1 TextBox". Text1 is the current name of the text box, and we will use that name throughout this text. The two tabs permit you to view the list of properties either alphabetically or grouped into categories. Text boxes have 43 properties that can be grouped into 7 categories, but we will use only two or three of them in this text. Use the up-arrow or down-arrow keys to glance through the list. The left column gives you the property name and the right column gives you the current setting of the property.

Alphabetic view

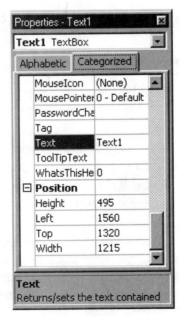

Categorized view

 Figure 4-5. Two views of the Properties window.

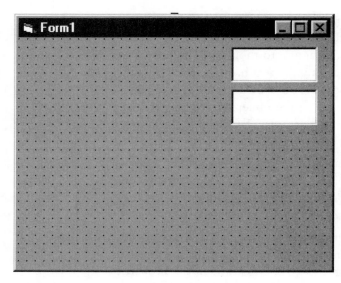

Figure 4-6. Two blank text boxes on the design form.

7. Move to the "Text" property with the up-arrow or down-arrow keys. Scroll up or down until the "Text" property is highlighted, as in one of the views in Figure 4-5.

8. Click-and-drag the "Text1" value, and press the "Delete" key. The text disappears from your textbox on the form. Now you are ready to enter data into the text box, which we will do later.

9. Create another text box by repeating steps 1, 7, and 8. Note that the name of the second text box is "Text2", and it will be the "Text2" value that you will delete in the properties box for the second text box.

10. Reposition each of the text boxes until your design form looks similar to Figure 4-6. We are ready to add the processing object, the Command Button.

COMMAND BUTTON Tutorial

1. Double-click on the command button icon to place a command button in the center of the form. The rectangular-shaped command button icon is the sixth icon in the Toolbox.

2. Be sure that the "Caption" property is highlighted in the Properties window.

3. Point to the property value "Command1". Click-and-drag to highlight "Command1", then type, "COMPUTE!". You may have also noticed that the letters appear on the command button as you entered them into the property value.

4. To check the command button's action, run the program. You do this in one of three ways. Either click the blue triangle on the toolbar that is below the menu bar command "Diagram", or select "Run" from the menu bar then select "Start" from the pull-down menu, or finally, press F5.

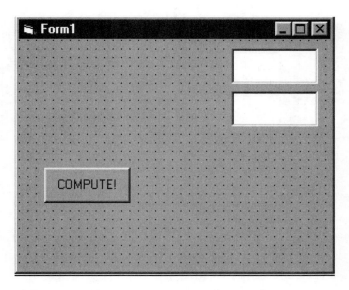

Figure 4-7. Command button added to the design form.

5. The command button appears to move in and out. In the next chapter, we will enter code in the command button that will produce the output of Gross Pay.

6. Reposition the command button so your form is similar to Figure 4-7.

PICTURE BOX Tutorial

1. Double-click on the picture box icon to place a picture box in the center of the form. The picture box icon is the second icon in the Toolbox. It contains a picture of the sun shining over a desert.

2. Run the program. Nothing happens and nothing will, no matter what you do. Although picture boxes look like text boxes, you cannot type in them. They are used to display output, as you will see in the next chapter when we complete the program for calculating Gross Pay.

3. Note that the picture box is the same color as the background, and the text box is white. That is an easy way to tell which is which. Another is to just click on the object and look at the first line of the Properties window. It will display "Properties-" then the type of object, such as "Picture1".

4. Resize and reposition the picture box so you form is similar to Figure 4-8.

LABEL Tutorial

1. Double-click on the label icon to place a label in the center of the form. The label icon, a large letter "A", is the third icon in the Toolbox.

2. Move the label next to the first text box on the design form.

3. The "Caption" property should already be highlighted in the Properties window. If not, scroll through the list until you come to the "Caption" property. Click-and-drag over the "Label1" property value, and type "Enter the Rate of Pay: ". Don't worry about the label scrolling in the property value box. You will also notice that the text also appears in the label as you type it into the property value.

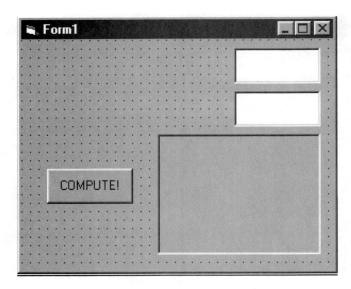

Figure 4-8. Picture box added to the design form.

4. Click on the label (next to the text box) to select it, then widen it until all the words are on the same line.

5. Make the label narrower until only the words occupy the label box.

6. Repeat step 1, making a second label with the property value of "Label2".

7. Move this label next to the second text box.

8. Click-and-drag over the "Label2" property value in the Properties window and type "Enter the number of Hours Worked:".

9. Resize the second label box using the same processes you did for the first one.

10. Run the program. Nothing happens with labels either. Their text is fixed once you enter it into the property value.

11. Now that you have used all four basic objects to create the user interface, your form should look like Figure 4-9.

12. You may wish to go to Section 4-3 and use the "Save" tutorial to save the Visual Basic project you just created. I would suggest a name like **Gross-Pay** which tells you immediately what the project is all about.

Congratulations! You have created two text boxes (one to input the value for *numRate* and one to input the value for *numHours*), a command button into which we will enter the program code (in the next chapter), and a picture box to display the output, *numGrossPay*. You are well on your way to creating your first program! There are just a few more items to present before that "magical" moment!

The next two sections cover controlling your programs and projects, and debugging your programs, but first a few helpful hints.

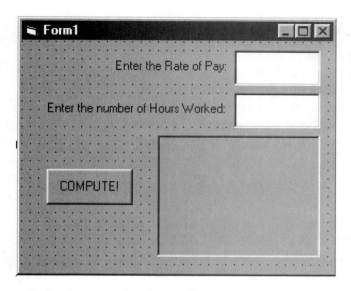

Figure 4-9. Labels placed in the design form.

1. When selecting the property value in the Property window, double-clicking has the same effect as clicking once and pressing the "Enter" key, or of using the click-and-drag method.

2. The form itself is also an object with properties. For instance, you can resize the form using the handles, or by using the maximize button on the title bar.

3. If you inadvertently double-click an object and a window containing two lines of text appears (the first line beginning with "Private Sub", just click the close button in the upper right corner. It is a code window and we cover it in Chapter 5.

Exercise 4-2

Retrieve the annotated flowcharts you did in Exercise 3-4. You are going to practice assigning objects to the flowchart symbols. Place the words for the correct object next to the flowchart symbols in each problem. In case you forgot what the problems were, here they are again.

1. Once a user has entered any two numbers, add the numbers together and display their sum.

2. After a person enters their first name and last name, print their entire name on one line.

3. Have a person enter their name and age, determine what a person's age would be ten years from now, then print their name and age in ten years.

4. Find the number of square yards of carpet needed to cover a room that is 12 feet by 15 feet. (area = length * width, and 1 square yard = 9 square feet).

5. Calculate the total bill when a customer buys any three items from a menu. (Use this data for a test case: lemonade for 75 cents, a cheeseburger for $1.25, and french fries for 90 cents.) Then print out each item with its associated cost, and the total cost. Remember that you should allow this program to calculate any three items selected from the menu.

4-3.   Controlling Programs and Projects

When using Microsoft Visual Basic, the term **project** refers to the combination of the user interface (objects and the form) and the programming code. The term **program** means a series of Visual Basic commands, assembled and arranged in order of execution, that are placed within the Command Button.

This section will give you steps to accomplish many recurring tasks involved with programming in Visual Basic such as creating, saving, or opening new or existing projects or programs.

Managing Your Programs

A. *Begin a new program* (from within the initial Visual Basic window)
1. Click on the Start icon (blue triangle) on the Toolbar.
   OR
1. Select "File" from the menu bar.
2. Select "New Project" from the pull-down menu.

B. *Save the current program on a disk*
1. Click on the Save icon (the picture of a microfloppy) on the Toolbar.
   OR
1. Select "File" from the menu bar.
2. Select "Save Project" from the pull-down menu.

NOTE: If an unsaved program is present, Visual Basic will prompt you to save it.

C. *Run a program* (from within the initial Visual Basic screen)
1. To prevent possible problems, save the program first.
2. Click on the Start icon (the blue triangle) on the Toolbar.
   OR
2. Press the "F5" key.

D. *Open a program stored on a disk*
1. Click on the Open Project icon (the yellow folder) on the Toolbar.
2. (Go to step 3).
   OR
1. "File" from the menu bar.
2. Select "Open Project" from the pull-down menu.
3. Click on one of the two tabs, "Existing" or "Recent".
4. If you selected "Existing", choose a folder for the "Look in:" box, type a file name into the "File name:" box, and press the "Enter" key. Alternately, you could double-click one of the filenames displayed in the Open Project window

E. *Obtain the programming code* (of an existing program)
1. Select "View" from the menu bar.

2. Select "Code" from the pull-down menu, and the code window appears.

   OR

1. Open the Project Explorer window.

2. Double-click on the form name.

3. Double-click on the object containing the program.

F. *Display the form* (of an existing program)

    1. Select "View" from the menu bar.

    2. Select "Object" from the pull-down menu.

        OR

    1. Hold down the "Shift" key and press the "F7" key.

G. *Display the Toolbox*

    1. Select "View" from the menu bar.

    2. Select "Toolbox" from the pull-down menu.

        OR

    1. Click the Toolbox icon (the crossed wrench and hammer) on the toolbar.

H. *Obtaining a printout of a program* (source code)

    1. Select "File" from the menu bar.

    2. Select "Print…" from the pull-down menu.

    3. Be sure that "Range" is "Current Module", and "Print What" has a check beside "Code".

    4. Click "OK".

I. *Obtaining a printout of the form*

    1. Hold down the "Alt" key and press the "Print Scrn" key. This copies the screen to the Microsoft Windows clipboard.

    2. Open Microsoft Word.

    3. Right click to get a pop-up menu.

    4. Select "Paste".

    5. Click on the Print icon (a printer) on the Toolbar.

        OR

    1. Place the statement "PrintForm" in the program where a record of the output is needed. This may or may not be at the end of the program.

■ Exercise 4-3

Once again, we will use the problems you have been working on in previous exercises.

1. Now that you have assigned the correct objects for the first problem in Exercise 4-2, place those objects in the design window and save the problem as a project name you can remember, i.e. **Exersize4_1** (or something similar).

2. Do the same process for problems 2 through 5, saving each as you go.

We will add programming code to each project in the next chapter.

4-4. Debugging Programs

Although you have yet to create a program (you did begin 5 projects), this section will provide you a few techniques for identifying and correcting processing and coding errors that are most likely to occur in your programs. This is especially true in the later chapters when the programs will become more complex, involving repetitive structures.

A **bug** is a glitch or an error in programming logic or syntax. A **logic error** is committed when you enter a valid command in your program, but it does not do what you expected it to do. Telling the computer to add two numbers when you really wanted to multiply them, or declaring a numeric variable when it was supposed to be a string variable, are examples of logic errors. Often, the command that contains the logic error is in the proper syntax. A **syntax error** occurs when you violated the rules for entering program commands in a particular programming language. A syntax error would be a problem in spacing, punctuation, spelling, and so on, i.e. PRIMT instead of PRINT, or Picture 1 instead of Picture1.

An interpreter or a compiler commonly identifies syntax errors. An **interpreter** is a software package that will check syntax *within a line of code* the second after you hit the Enter key at the end of that line. A **compiler** waits until you have entered the entire program, then checks all lines of code for syntax errors prior to executing the program. Visual Basic uses a compiler.

When done properly, annotated flowcharts are supposed to catch logic problems. The Visual Basic compiler will catch syntax problems line-by-line after you try to execute the program. Then why do you need a debugger and debugging techniques?

The unfortunate truth is that you, me, and hundreds-of-thousands of other programmers will often try to take shortcuts by not doing a properly annotated flowchart. Logic errors are then combined with syntax errors to produce a frustrating, sometimes multi-hour, debugging exercise.

If there are two pieces of advice you must take with you from this section, they are: (1) *be very through in your annotated flowchart*; and (2) *never, never change the order of your lines of code just to see if it may make your program run*. It will only jumble the logic even worse, often to the point that you cannot even understand your own program! Go back to the flowchart and make sure that your program has the same logic, the same variables, and the same processes that were stated on your "map."

A. *"Stepping" through an existing program from program start*

1. If you have any text boxes that require input, do it at this time.

2. Press the "F8" key.

3. The first executable statement will be highlighted. If the statement being executed requires input, you have to enter the input value(s) and press the "Enter" key before continuing.

4. Press F8 to execute each highlighted statement.

NOTE: You will probably need to occasionally hold down the "Alt" key and press the "Tab" key to toggle back and forth between the code and the interface (form with objects).

B. *"Stepping" through an existing program from a point in the program*
   1. You should have entered values in text boxes before executing "Run".
   2. Hold down the "Ctrl" key and press the "F8" key.
      OR
   2. Select "Debug" from the menu bar.
   3. Select "Run To Cursor" from the pull-down menu.

C. *Inserting a breakpoint (to stop a program at a specified time)* Line)
   1. Place the cursor on the desired line.
   2. Press the "F9" key to highlight the line in red.
   3. Run the program. Execution will stop at the breakpoint (before the highlighted line).

D. *Deleting a breakpoint*
   1. Place the cursor on the highlighted (red) line.
   2. Press the "F9" key.

E. *Deleting all breakpoints*
   1. Select "Debug" from the menu bar.
   2. Select "Clear All Breakpoints" from the pull-down menu.
      OR
   1. Hold down the "Shift" and "Alt" keys and press the "F9" key.

F. *Continue executing a program that has been suspended.*
   1. Press the "F5" key.

NOTE: Each time an attempt is made to change a suspended program in a way that would prevent it from continuing, Visual Basic displays a dialog box warning that the program will have to be restarted from the beginning. It gives you an option to cancel the attempted change, but you will often want to accept the change.

G. *Determine the value of an expression or variable during program Execution*
   1. Place "Picture1.Print" statements after every line of code that changes the value of a variable or of an expression.
   2. Check the final output for a record of changes (or the lack there-of) for the variables or expressions.
      OR
   2. Step through the program using the "F8" key. As you pass a line of code that should have changed the value of a variable or an expression, you can toggle between the output screen and the program by holding down the "Alt" key while you press the "Tab" key.

NOTE: You may have to increase the size of your picture box prior to program execution to see the increased number of displayed lines in the box.

Exercise 4-4

1. a. What is a bug, in computer terms?

   b. Can a bug be eliminated? How?

2. a. What are the two different types of errors a programmer may commit?

   b. Define each.

3. a. How do you "step through a program"?

   b. What are the advantages of using this technique to debug a program?

4. a. How can you check the value of a variable during program execution?

   b. What does it mean when the value remains the same, or there is no value indicated for the variable at all?

5. a. Define the terms compiler and interpreter as they pertain to computers.

   b. Which is used by the Visual Basic programming language?

   c. Will you see syntax errors identified as you write the code for your Visual Basic program?

CHAPTER 5

SEQUENCE

5-1. Introduction

You have learned how to break down a problem with I-P-O diagramming. You know how to convert that diagram into a flowchart, then trace, desk-check, and annotate the flowchart. Finally, you learned how to select the correct objects for input, processing and output, and create the interface. Now we tie them all together with programming.

From the previous chapter, you learned that Microsoft Visual Basic uses the term **project** to refer to the combination of the user interface (objects in the form) and the programming code. In this text, the term **program** means a series of Visual Basic commands, assembled and arranged in order of execution, that are placed within the Command Button. The program we will be entering into the command button is also known as **source code**.

We begin the programming process by learning the various parts of the code window. This is accomplished by once again using a tutorial. Then, using the Gross Pay example, we will introduce the various means of input, processing, and output in later sections of this chapter.

If you saved the Gross Pay example project that you designed in Chapter 4, you can use that project now (it was probably saved as **GrossPay**). Otherwise, you must do steps 1 through 9 to recreate the interface.

Accessing the Code Window

1. Open Visual Basic 6.0.
2. Click on "Standard.EXE" to start a new project.
3. Place a text box near the top center of the form.
4. Place a second text box just below that one.
5. Place a command button to the right of the text boxes.
6. Place a picture box below all the items.
7. Resize the picture box so it covers the entire bottom portion of the form.
8. Place a label stating "Enter employee's rate of pay:" next to the first text box.
9. Place a label stating, "Enter number of hours worked:" next to the second text box.

NOTE: Once your form is similar to Figure 4-9, proceed to Step 10.

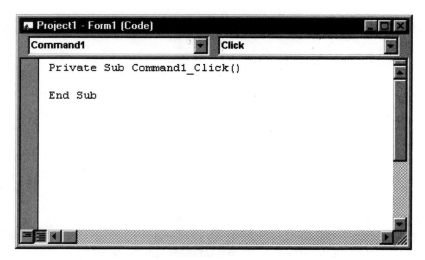

Figure 5-1. The code window.

10. Double-click on the command button. A window, called the **code window**, appears, as shown in Figure 5-1. Just below the title bar are two drop-down list boxes. The left box is called the Object box because it contains a list of objects. The right box is called the Procedure box because it contains a list of procedures. We will not use either one in this text.

NOTE: To hide the code window, press the right mouse button to get a pop-up menu, then click on Hide. You can also hide it by clicking on the icon at the left side of the title bar and clicking on Close. To view hidden code, select View from the menu bar and Code from the pull-down menu.

11. Press the "Tab" key. The insertion point should be about under the "a" in "Private".

NOTE: Although not necessary to program execution, we will be using **indenting** as a means of keeping track of the structure and programming constructs in a program.

12. Your first line of code to enter will be:

```
Picture1.Cls
```

NOTE: Before you begin entering code, there are certain words, such as Sub, End, and False, that have special meanings in Visual Basic. These words are referred to as **keywords** or **reserved words.** The Visual Basic editor automatically capitalizes the first letter of a keyword and displays the word in blue. Therefore, you can begin typing without using upper case letters until you get to a variable name. Visual Basic will capitalize the commands for you.

Press the "Enter" key after it is complete. The line of code should have been accepted, and the insertion point moved to the next line under the "P" in "Picture", ready for the next line of code.

NOTE: Picture1.Cls should be *the first executable statement in all your programs.* It clears the picture box of all output from a previous run of this program or other programs.

---

13. The text input (to a text box) will be a considered by the computer as a string constant and will therefore be ineligible for use in a calculation. However, as programmer wizards, we can change the string constant to a numeric constant and use it in our calculation of Gross Pay. We do this by using a built-in function to change the text (string) input to a number (numeric). This function is called the **Val** function. For instance, the expression **Val(Text1.Text)** would change an input of *"7.00"*, a string constant entered into the first text box, into *7.00*, a numeric constant.

14. Next, we must assign the numeric value that will be entered into the first text box (7.00 in our example) to the numeric variable *numRate*. The proper form for value assignment is **Let variable = expression**. The variable goes on the left, an equal sign next, then an expression on the right. As you remember from Chapter 3, the equal sign *assigns the value of the expression on the right to the variable on the left.* Therefore the next line of code for you to type is:

```
Let numRate = Val(Text1.Text)
```

15. You are probably ahead of me, but we need to assign the value to be entered into the second text box, *Text2*, to the variable *numHours*. So, next you will type:

```
Let numHours = Val(Text2.Text)
```

Great! The two inputs are taken care of.

16. Processing is usually dealt with in much the same manner; variable on the left and expression on the right. As you recall, the objective of the problem was to determine a value for the variable, numGrossPay. To do that, we had to multiply numRate times numHours. Therefore, the next statement for you to enter will be:

```
Let numGrossPay = numRate * numHours
```

Processing commands are complete!

17. Output is next, and you already know that we use the picture box to display output. The correct format for an output command is **Picture1.Print variable**. Since we need to display the value we have found for numGrossPay, the final line of code is:

```
Picture1.Print numGrossPay
```

Hold it! Don't execute that program quite yet! Take a look at the program. You should be able to see at a glance, from looking at the code, that the program will be executed just as you planned in your flowchart. Your program should look exactly like the one in Figure 5-2.

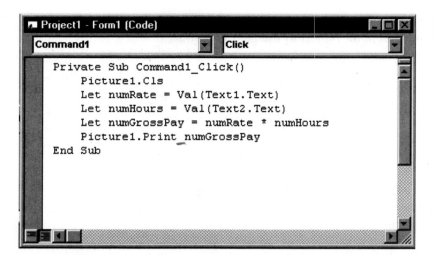

after

Figure 5-2. Gross Pay program with text boxes.

NOTE: Code windows have many features of word processors. For instance, the *cut, copy, paste, find, undo,* and *redo* operations can be carried out with the sixth through eleventh icons of the Toolbar. These operations, and several others, can also be initiated from the Edit menu.

OK. RUN YOUR PROGRAM!

- Press the "F5" key or click the blue triangle on the Toolbar.
- Enter **7.00** into the first text box.
- Press the "Tab" key.
- Enter **40** in the second text box.
- Press the "Tab" key.
- The command button is now highlighted. Press "Enter".
- If you see **280** in the picture box, you did it!! If not, that is why you were given the debugging section in the previous chapter.

What does the flowchart for this example look like? It hasn't changed much from Chapter 3, Figure 3-4. We added another input flowchart symbol to obtain the employee's name. The revised flowchart is like the one in Figure 5-3.

After you check out the flowchart, it is time to introduce you to the various input commands.

5-2. Input (Text Boxes, Input Boxes, and Reading Data from Data Files)

Text Boxes

A *text box* is a Visual Basic object that is used for input from the user interface. You have already experienced the use of text boxes for *numerical input* with the help of the *Val* function. Obviously, text boxes can also be used for *textual input*. For example, it would be good to know for whom we were calculating gross pay. Since we do not know which employee will be calculated first, we use a

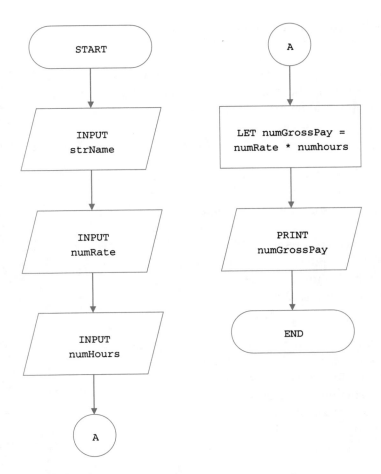

Figure 5-3. Revised flowchart for the Gross Pay example.

string variable for the name, *strName*. A text box is used to input the employee's name. Keeping the *variable = expression* format, the line of code would be:

```
Let strName = Text1.Text
```

Note that the *Val* function is *not* included in the statement because we want a string constant not a numeric constant.

Now that we know what the correct code would be, we have to go back to the flowchart and insert a new input symbol. Where would you place the new input in Figure 3-9?

Yes, right after the "START" and before the input symbol containing the words "INPUT numRate". After the name is entered, you would also have to include it as output. Where will you place the new output symbol?

Correct again. Immediately before you display the value for gross pay. So, placing it after "Let numGrossPay =..." and before "Print numGrossPay" lets you know which employee receives the gross pay.

You must revise the flowchart as you revise the program. That way, your documentation—the flowchart—remains a reliable "map" of your program logic. Where do the new lines of code go in your program?

Right again. The input box command goes after the first line of executable code, "Picture1.Cls" and before the input code line, "Let numRate = Val(Text1.Text). Excellent!

The output command, which will be covered later in this chapter, would be:

```
Picture1.Print strName
```

It would go after the "Let numGrossPay..." command and before the other "Picture1.Print..." command. You are getting the knack of program planning, object selection, programming commands, and program documentation.

Input Boxes

Normally, a text box is used to obtain input described by a label. Sometimes we want just one piece of input and would rather not have a text box and label stay on the screen forever. The problem can be solved with an *input box*.

An *input box* is a Visual Basic object that pops up as a result of a command entered into a program. After the user enters a response to the input box and presses the *Enter* key (or clicks *OK*), the response is assigned to the variable.

Input boxes can be used in conjunction with text boxes, or as a substitute for text boxes. The format for an input box command is:

```
variable = InputBox ("prompt", "input box title")
```

If we used an input box to obtain the employee's name, we would not have to alter the current design of the user interface (Figure 4-9), nor would the input box remain on the interface. It disappears after the input is accepted. Therefore, we can place the input box command after the "Picture1..." command and before the "Let numRate..." command, and not alter our form design. The command would appear as:

```
Let strName = InputBox("Enter the employee's name:", "Employee Name")
```

NOTE: When you typed the parenthesis following the word InputBox, the editor displays a line containing the general form of the InputBox statement. This feature is called Quick Info. Optional parameters are surrounded by brackets. All the parameters in the general form of the InputBox statement are optional except for the prompt.

This is a much longer programming line than you have seen before, but it works very well. When the program is run, the input box looks like Figure 5-4.

Now that you have added the input box command and picture box output command (for name), your program should look like Figure 5-5. (You will not be able to see the entire code for the input box command unless you scroll to the right or maximize the coding window.)

Figure 5-4. Input box for the employee's name.

```
Project1 - Form1 (Code)
Command1                          Click

Private Sub Command1_Click()
    Picture1.Cls
    Let strName = InputBox("Enter the employee's name", Name)
    Let numRate = Val(Text1.Text)
    Let numHours = Val(Text2.Text)
    Let numGrossPay = numRate * numHours
    Picture1.Print strName
    Picture1.Print numGrossPay
End Sub
```

Figure 5-5. Input box code with additional picture box output.

Many programming situations require multiple, recurring input to the same variable, especially when using a programming structure called loops. We will cover loops later in the text. You can expect to see more input boxes at that time, as well as more of the following customized input.

Reading Data from Data Files

This methodology is the last of the input techniques we will cover. It is a means of obtaining input data from an external source.

Reading data from files requires two things. First, it requires that an external data file, containing numeric and/or string constants, exist prior to program execution. A file can have either one item per line or many items (separated by commas) can be listed on the same line. Usually, related items are grouped together on a line. Let's prepare a data file for the computer to read using the Gross Pay example.

1. Open Microsoft Windows' Notepad. (It is in the "Accessories" folder in "Programs".)

2. Enter the following data: **"Eric Gregary", 7.00, 40** (Be sure to include the quotes around the name to signify that it is a string constant, and the commas to separate the data elements.)

3. Save the file as "PAYDATA", one word.

Secondly, after creating a data file to be read, we must have the correct commands to use in the program. These statements must open the file, obtain the data, and close the file. Those are the steps we will execute next.

4. Open the "PAYDATA" file by entering an Open statement into the Gross Pay program that will *Read* the *Data* from the Notepad file. The correct format for the command is **Open "FILENAME.TXT" For Input As #n** where *FILENAME* is the name of the data file, *.TXT* is a file extension that means *text* file, and *n* is the *reference number* for the data file.

NOTE: We have only one file, so it will be #1. If you had additional files, they could be given any number from 1 to 255.

5. Enter the following command immediately after "Picture1.Cls":

```
Open "PAYDATA.TXT" For Input As #1
```

This procedure is referred to as "Opening a file for input." It establishes a link between the computer and the disk drive for reading the data file.

NOTE: You will have to alter the Open statement to tell it where the file PAYDATA.TXT is located if it is not on the same drive as your program. For instance, if the file is in the root directory of a diskette in drive "A", then the line should read **Open "A:\PAY-DATA.TXT" For Input As #1.** If the file is located in the subdirectory (that is folder) VB6 of the "C" drive, then the statement should be **Open "C:\VB6\PAYDATA.TXT" For Input As #1.**

6. Now we need to read the data in the data file one data item at a time, from left to right, using *Input #n, Variable* statements. The next line of code would be:

```
Input #1, strName
```

The statement says, "Input from data file #1 the value that will be assigned to the variable *strName*."

NOTE: Visual Basic *automatically keeps track* of which piece of data has been read, and which is next. Now that "Eric Gregary" has been assigned to *strName*, the next piece of data to be read is 7.00. Unless a special command is entered in the program, Visual Basic considers the string "Eric Gregary" as having already been read, and it *will not* be used again.

7. Add the code for the next two input lines. It will be:

```
Input #1, numRate
Input #1, numHours
```

NOTE: Data being read *must be in the same order and of the same type* as the variables to which they are being assigned, i.e. a string constant into a string variable, and a numeric constant into a numeric variable.

8. We are done reading data from the data file, so we need to close it. This is accomplished by using a close statement in the simple form of **Close #n.** The final statement to add is:

```
Close #1
```

9. Your modified Gross Pay program should look like Figure 5-6.

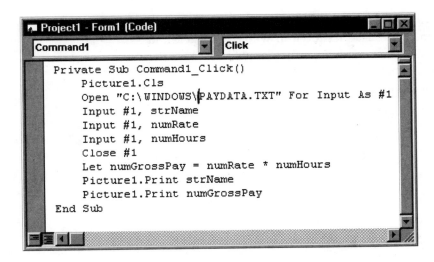

Figure 5-6. Reading data from an external file.

What about the flowchart for these examples? Did it change when we switched input objects from text box to input box? Did it change again when we read the data from an external file? In every case, the answer is, "No, the flowchart did not change." It has remained the same through every change of input format.

Therefore, you need to know which programming construct does what, for all input formats accomplish nearly the same thing, but in slightly different ways. It is this slight difference that allows you to customize the program to the exact needs of the user. For example, if the data can be obtained through electronic files already in existence, then read the input from the external file. Do not have the user re-enter the data.

You will find that the same holds true for many other constructs. There may be many different ways to accomplish relatively the same thing, but knowing which is the precise construct for the scenario will make you a much better programmer.

Will the flowchart for problem using a text box look different than a flowchart for a problem using an input box? Time for a little practice with text boxes, input boxes, and reading data from a file.

Exercise 5-2

Having completed the input tutorials in this section, you are ready to modify your standard problems with the new programming constructs. Note the wording in each problem, for they have all changed.

1. Start your program, then ask the user to enter any two numbers, one number at a time. Add the numbers together, then display their sum.

2. After you start your program, have the user enter his or her first name and a space, then enter their last name. Print their entire name on one line.

3. Create a data file on your working disk ("A" drive) that has the name and age of a person, and name that file PROGDATA.TXT. Using that file, determine what the person's age would be ten years from now, then print their name and their age in ten years.

4. Note: Do not use a Text Box for input in this program. Start your program, then have a user enter the size of a room in whole feet, then find and display the number of square yards of carpet needed to cover the room. (area = length * width, and 1 square yard = 9 square feet).

5. Create a program that will produce a customer receipt using the items and costs listed below. It must print out the items, their asssociated costs, and the total of their order.

Item	Cost
lg. dietcoke	1.25
turkeyclub	3.75
veg.soup	1.95

5-3. Processing (Variables, Functions, and Program Documentation)

Variables

You already use *meaningful variables* in your processing, and name them according to a strict *naming convention*. There are a few more helpful rules and points you need to know about variables.

1. If an input statement (Text box or Input box) is looking for a string and finds a number, it *automatically accepts the number as a string.* Using our Gross Pay example, let's say you forgot to use the Val function to change the text input to a number. Visual Basic would readily accept 7 as the employee's name, "7".

2. If the input statement is looking for a number and it finds a string, Visual Basic *automatically assigns the value 0 (zero) to the numeric variable,* and it can result in the error message, "Type mismatch". In the Gross Pay example, if you tried to enter the employee's name, "Eric", into *numRate,* Visual Basic would assign the value 0 to *numRate.*

3. A string constant used in a data statement or for data input does not necessarily have to be enclosed by quotation marks. However, for the sake of consistency and mutual understanding, we will *use quotation marks around all string constants.*

4. When obtaining input from an external file, *there must be as many or fewer input statements as there are data elements in the external file.* Seven read statements will require seven or more data elements. Otherwise, a box will appear displaying the message, "Input past end of file".

5. *Numeric data in a text box, input box, or external file must be a numeric constant* (computer number). It cannot be a variable or an expression. For example, the fraction ½ or the expression **2 + 3** are not acceptable, even though they are made up of numeric constants.

6. *Before being assigned a value, numeric variables have a value of zero, and string variables have a value of null.* The numeric value zero is less than one and more than minus 1. The string value of null has no value whatsoever; it truly means nothing exists. This is true of all variables in a program, whether declared at the beginning of the program or created during program execution.

Functions

If you take a full course in Visual Basic, you will find that there are many, many more functions than what we will be using in this text. For the sake of simplicity and understanding, we will limit ourselves to a few numeric and string functions.

A. *Numeric Functions: Sqr, Int, Round*

The function **Sqr** calculates the square root of a number. The function **Int** finds the greatest integer (whole number) less than or equal to a number. In other words, Int discards the decimal part of positive numbers, and rounds up on negative numbers. The value of **Round (n, r)** is the number n rounded to r decimal places. The parameter r can be omitted. If so, n is rounded to a whole number. Some examples of these numeric functions are:

Sqr(9) is 3	Int(2.7) is 2	Round(2.7) is 3
Sqr(0) is 0	Int(3) is 3	Round(2.317, 2) is 2.32
Sqr(2) is 1.414214	Int(-2.7) is -3	Round(2.317, 1) is 2.3

NOTE: The terms inside the parenthesis can be either numbers as shown above, numeric variables, or numeric expressions. Expressions are evaluated first to produce the input.

The square root function will not calculate the square root of a negative number. Instead, you will get the error message, "Invalid procedure call or argument."

B. *String Functions: Left, Mid, Right, UCase*

The functions **Left, Mid,** and **Right** are used to extract characters from the left end, middle, and right end of a string. Suppose *strVar* is a string and m and n are positive integers. Then *Left(strVar, n)* is the string consisting of the first n characters of *strVar*, and *Right(strVar, n)* is the string consisting of the last n characters of *strVar*. *Mid(strVar, m, n)* is the string consisting of n characters of *strVar*, beginning with the mth character. **UCase(strVar)** is the string *strVar* with all of its lower case letters capitalized. Some examples of each of these are:

Left("fanatic", 3) is "fan	Right("fanatic", 3) is "tic"
Left("12/15/99", 3) is "12/"	Right("12/15/99", 3) is "/99"
Mid("fanatic", 5, 1) is "t"	Mid("12/15/99", 4, 2) is "15"
UCase("Disk") is "DISK"	UCase("12three") is "12THREE"
UCase(strAns) when strAns = "y" is "Y"	

Visual Basic has a function called *LCase* that is analogous to *UCase*. **LCase** converts all uppercase letters in a string to lower case letters. Which one you use is of no consequence. However, for the sake of consistency, it is best if you pick one of them and do not change your style within a program.

If n is greater than the length of *strVar*, then the value of *Left(strVar, n)* will be the entire string *strVar*. A similar result holds true for *Mid* and *Right*.

NOTE: Like the numeric functions discussed earlier, *Left*, *Mid*, *Right*, and *UCase* can be evaluated for variables and expressions.

C. *String-related Numeric Function: Len*

The function *Len* operates on a string, but produces a number. **Len** is used to return the number of characters in a string. The value of *Len(strVar)* is the number of characters in *strVar*. Some examples of *Len* are:

Len("Appalachian") is 11   Len("Just a moment") is 13

Len(" ") is 1   Len(strVar) when strVar = "Croissant" is 9

Program Documentation

Program documentation is a record of the logic flow, decisions made, variables used, user interface, and other pertinent aspects of the processes and content of a program. Documentation includes the annotated flowchart, program code, design form, and hard-copy output, even when that output is a printout of a soft-copy display.

There are a number of great reasons to document your programs and programming effort, not the least of which is your personal use as a study guide and future programming resource. Nonetheless, students often dismiss documentation as a waste of time. However, please resist the shortcuts and fully document your programs. You can help yourself become a better programmer through complete documentation.

Documentation is either *internal* or *external* to the program. **Internal documentation** consists of comments placed in the source code that specify the intent of a program, the purpose of the variables, the nature of the data in the files, and the tasks performed by individual portions of the program. In general, comments are anything that will help you understand the program now, as you are programming, and many months in the future when you use it again either alone or as a starting point for another program.

Comments are entered into the program code using either a *Rem* statement (short for *Remark*) or by using an apostrophe ('). In either case, once *Rem* or an apostrophe is used, everything after that, *on that line,* will be totally disregarded by the computer.

The use of the *Rem* is restrictive; it can be used only at the beginning of a statement, and nowhere else. The apostrophe, on the other hand, has no such restriction. It can be used at the beginning of a statement or in the middle of a statement. Since where an apostrophe is used makes no difference in its effect, the apostrophe is often chosen over the *Rem* statement.

Comments will appear as green text on the screen.

The program for our Gross Pay example, with full internal documentation (comments), is shown in Figure 5-7.

External documentation is everything other than comments in the source code. It is the flowchart, the program itself, the interface, any and all objects, etc. When combined with internal documentation, you the programmer should be able to easily explain to anyone the precise thoughts and processes involved in your program.

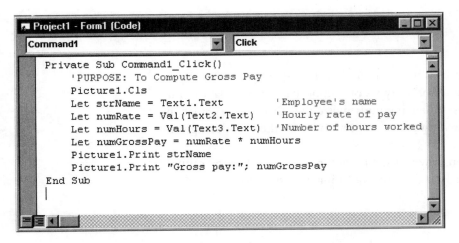

```
Project1 - Form1 [Code]                                    _ □ ×
Command1              ▼    Click                           ▼
Private Sub Command1_Click()
    'PURPOSE: To Compute Gross Pay
    Picture1.Cls
    Let strName = Text1.Text          'Employee's name
    Let numRate = Val(Text2.Text)     'Hourly rate of pay
    Let numHours = Val(Text3.Text)    'Number of hours worked
    Let numGrossPay = numRate * numHours
    Picture1.Print strName
    Picture1.Print "Gross pay:"; numGrossPay
End Sub
```

Figure 5-7. Internal documentation example.

Exercises 5-3

In Exercises 1 through 16, find the value of the given function.

1. Ucase("McD's") "MCD'S"   2. Sqr(54) 7.734

3. Int(10.75) 10   4. Left("harp", 2) ha

5. Sqr(3 * 12) 6   6. Int(9–2) 7

7. Round(3.1279, 3) 3.128   8. Round(-2.6) –3

9. Left("ABCD", 2) AB   10. Mid("ABCDE", 2, 3) BCD

11. Mid("shoe", 4, 1) e   12. Ucase("$2 bi") $2 BI

13. Len("shoe") 4   14. Len("s" & Left("help", 2)) Len("s" & "he")
                                                                 Len("she") = 3

15. Right("snow", 3) 3   16. Right("123", 1) 3

In Exercises 17 through 32, find the value of the given function where
a and *b* are numeric variables, *c* and *d* are string variables; *a* = 5, *b* = 3, *c* =
"Lullaby", and *d* = "lab".

17. Len(d) = 3   18. Sqr(4 + a) 3

19. Int(-a / 2) – 3   20. UCase(d) LAB

21. Round(a / b, 2) 1.67   22. Round(a + .5) 5.5

23. Sqr(a -5) 0   24. Int(b * .5) 1

25. Left(c, Len(d)) = "Lul"   26. Mid(c, a, 3) "aby"

27. Mid(c, a–b, 2 * a)   28. Left(d, b–2) L

29. Ucase(c) LULLABY   30. Len(c & Left(d, 2)) = 9

31. Right(c, 2) By   32. Right("Sky" & d, 5) KyLab

5-4.   Output (Displayed Output, Printed Output, and Message Boxes)

Displayed Output

You have already experienced using a Picture box to display program output. However, there are a number of other types of output that are essential to Visual Basic programming. These other methods will either provide a permanent record of your efforts, or provide a temporary reminder for the user during program execution.

In case you have forgotten how to use the Picture box for soft-copy output, see Chapter 4 for the tutorial on creating and using a Picture box.

Printed Output

There are a number of reasons to obtain hard-copy (printed) output, ranging from debugging a program to creating a programming portfolio. The timing of the output is also important, for some of the following are designed to provide a printed record of your efforts, some provide the information requested by the user, while the last one is more of a temporary reminder than a permanent record.

A. *Program Results Printout*

You print text on a sheet of paper in the printer much the same way you display text in a picture box. Visual Basic treats the printer as an object named *Printer*. If *strName* is a string expression, then

```
Printer.Print strName, OR Printer.Print "Name: "; strName
```

sends *strName* to the printer in exactly the same way *Picture1.Print* sends output to a picture box. Likewise, you can use semicolons to concatenate, and commas to print in print zones. If you would like to start a new page, the command is:

```
Printer.NewPage
```

The Microsoft Windows Print Manager usually waits until an entire page has been completed before starting to print. To avoid losing information, execute the following statement when you are finished printing:

```
Printer.EndDoc
```

B. *Program (Source Code) Printout*

Under normal circumstances, your instructor will want a hard copy of the program code. It is easy to provide this to him or her. Using the menu bar, select **File,** and from the pull-down menu select **Print.** You will see a combination box which looks like Figure 5-7. Be sure that "Current Module" and "Code" have been selected, then press "OK".

C. *Design Form Printout*

If you look at Figure 5-8, you will see a label directly above "Code" named "Form Image." If you check that box and click on "OK", you will get a printout of the design form. You may also be required to hand this in to your instructor.

There is one more method of obtaining hard-copy output, and it is the only way to print out anything that appears on the screen.

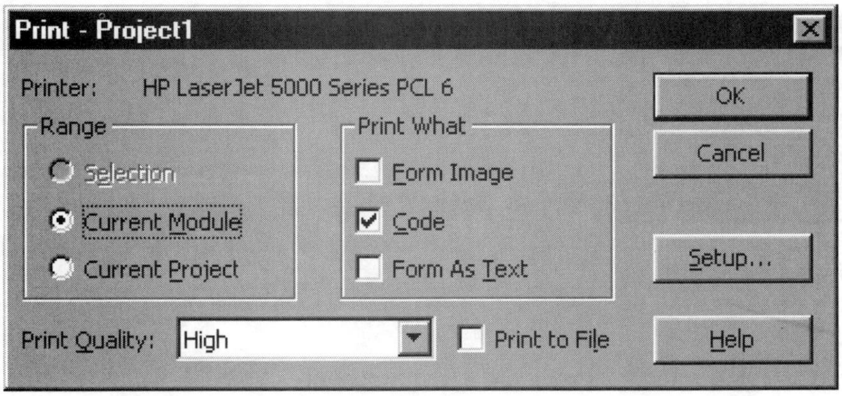

```
Print - Project1                                    [X]

Printer:    HP LaserJet 5000 Series PCL 6           ┌──────────┐
                                                    │    OK    │
┌─Range──────────────┐  ┌─Print What─────────────┐  └──────────┘
│  ○  Selection      │  │  ☐  Form Image         │  ┌──────────┐
│  ◉  Current Module │  │  ☑  Code               │  │  Cancel  │
│  ○  Current Project│  │  ☐  Form As Text       │  └──────────┘
└────────────────────┘  └────────────────────────┘
                                                    ┌──────────┐
                                                    │  Setup...│
Print Quality:  │High            ▼│  ☐ Print to File└──────────┘
                                                    ┌──────────┐
                                                    │   Help   │
                                                    └──────────┘
```

FIGURE 5-8. Print screen to print source code.

D. *Screen Capture Printout*

The screen capture printout method is used to print literally anything that appears on the screen. To accomplish this task:

1. Have Microsoft Word running simultaneously with Visual Basic.

2. Once you have both icons shown on the task bar (the last line on the screen), display whatever it is you want to print.

3. Hold down the Ctrl key and press the PrintScrn button once. You will not see anything happen, but a copy of the screen display was placed into the Microsoft clipboard.

4. Switch to a new document in Microsoft Word.

5. Click the right mouse button and a pop-up menu will appear.

6. Select "Paste" and a copy of the screen display will appear (be embedded) in that document.

7. Print the document using the Printer icon on the Toolbar or select File from the menu bar, and Print from the pull-down menu.

This method of printing can be used to provide you (and your instructor) a permanent copy of a message box.

Message Boxes

Sometimes you want to grab the user's attention with a brief message such as "Correct" or "Nice try, but no cigar!" This mission is easily accomplished with a *message box*. A *message box* is an object that pops up when a message box statement is executed in a program. The message box remains on the screen until the user has acknowledged it by pressing the *Enter* key or clicking on *OK*. The format for a message box command is:

```
MsgBox prompt, , title
```

Remember that unless you use the *Ctrl-PrintScrn* method of copying, pasting, and printing, the message box disappears for good until it is once again invoked by the program. There is no other means of obtaining a permanent output from a message box. An example of a message box is shown at Figure 5-9.

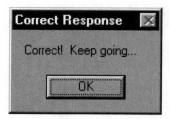

Figure 5-9. Example of a message box.

Which of the preceding constructs you select to provide the required output will depend on two things: when the output is created, and the nature of the output.

You can obtain a printout of whatever is displayed on the monitor by using the key combination of *Ctrl-PrintScrn*.

The *Printer.Print* command can give you a line-by-line printout during program execution, or, if used at the end of program, it can provide you a printout of the final results of the program.

As previously stated, the *MsgBox* command creates a message box that is very temporary. Until its message has been acknowledged, the program will not continue to execute.

Finally, a copy of the source code and/or the design form are important for program documentation, whether in an academic or work setting.

Exercises 5-4

1. Write a program to produce Table 5-1. (The amounts are given in millions of dollars.) The name, sport, salary or winnings, and endorsements for the four people should be contained in a data file. The totals should be computed by the program.

Athlete	Sport	Salary or Winnings	Endorsements	Total
M. Jordan	basketball	29.3	193.2	222.5
E. Holyfield	boxing	110.3	7.5	117.8
A. Agassi	tennis	11.3	63.5	74.8
W. Gretsky	hockey	36.8	31.5	68.3

Table 5-1 1990–96 earnings (in millions) of athletes.

2. Write a program to calculate the amount of a waiter's tip given the amount of the bill and the percentage tip. The output should be a complete sentence that reiterates the inputs and gives the resulting tip. For example, if $20 and 15% are the inputs, then the output might read "A 15 percent tip on 20 dollars is 3 dollars."

3. Design a form with two text boxes labeled "Name" and "Phone number". Then write an event procedure that shows a message box stating "Be sure to include the area code!" before entering data in the second text box.

CHAPTER 6

SELECTION

6-1.   Introduction

Selection is the second most important process in programming. Sequence is first, for if statements are out of sequence, the program rarely runs. Given that statements are in the correct order, the next significant consideration is giving the computer a means of choosing the most appropriate alternative among different options.

Selection allows a program to determine one, *and only one*, course of action from two or more alternatives based on which alternative matches the condition. Once the selection has been made, processing continues according to the parameters established by the selected alternative.

The selection process is the decision maker for the computer. It will help you decide:

- Which number is bigger?
- Did the user wish to continue processing or quit?
- Is the password the user entered correct?

These and many, many other decisions are appropriate for computer programming when using variations of *If / End If* or *Select Case* statements, which are presented next.

6-2.   IF / END IF

The first programming construct we will explore is commonly referred to as an *IF statement*, or an *If block*. An **If / End If block** allows a program to decide on a course of action based on whether a certain condition is *True* or *False*. The format for a coded *If* block is:

```
If condition Then
        takeAction1
Else
        takeAction2
End If
```

Basically, the computer checks the condition to see if it is true, and if it is, carries out its action. Once that action has been completed, it skips to the statement following the *End If*. If the first condition is not true, then *Else*'s action is carried out.

When used in a flowchart, like that of our Gross Pay example, the *If* block segment's structure would appear like Figure 6-1.

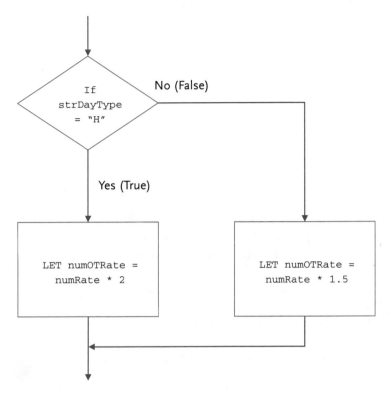

Figure 6-1. If block example.

Figure 6-1 shows that we needed to determine whether the employee did or did not work on a holiday. The source code for the *If block* in Figure 6-1 would be:

```
If UCase(strDayType) = "H" Then    'H = Holiday, OT = Overtime
    Let numOTRate = numRate * 2    'Double-time for holidays
Else
    Let numOTRate = numRate * 1.5 'Time-and-a-half normal OT
End If
```

The *Else* part of an *If* block can be omitted when *takeAction2* will merely carry on with the main program rather than execute a different action. This important type of If block is demonstrated in the next example.

```
If numHours > 40 Then       'OT = Anything over 40 hrs
    Let numOTHours = numHours - 40
End If
```

There is no need to calculate *numOTHours* when the employee has no overtime. Therefore, the program will skip any consideration of overtime rate when *numHours* is less than or equal to 40. The flowchart segment for an *IF / End If* block that does not have an *Else* consideration would be like Figure 6-2.

An *If* block can also use one or more *logical operators* in its condition, i.e.:

```
If numHours > 40 AND numHours <= 50 Then
    Let numOTRate = numOTRate * 1.5
End If
```

The flowchart for this example would be almost an exact copy of Figure 6-2. You need only add "AND numHours <= 50" inside the diamond.

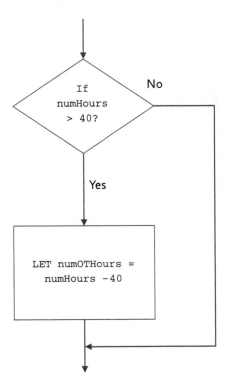

Figure 6-2. *If* block example without an *Else* consideration.

When comparing string input to a string condition, the use of the **UCase** string function is highly recommended. For example, assume that the user had been asked if he or she wished to have union dues automatically deducted from their pay. The response was "y". The correct If block condition would be:

```
If UCase(strAns) = "Y" Then
        Let numGrossPay = numGrossPay - numDues
End If
```

If you had not included the *UCase* function in the condition, the computer would compare "y" to "Y", determine that they are not equal (the condition is *False*), and fail to deduct the union dues from the employee's pay.

Finally, there are a few instances when you would need to place an *If* block inside another *If* block. These constructs are called **nested If blocks**. Care should be taken to make sure you need nested *If* blocks to accomplish your programming objective. In the following example, values for condition2 will be eligible for consideration if condition1 is met first. The generic structure is given on the left and an example from our Gross Pay problem is on the right.

```
If cond1 Then                If numHours > 40 Then
    If cond2 Then                If UCase(strDayType) = "H" Then
        takeAction1                  Let numRate = numRate * 2
    End If                       End If
End If                       End If
```

For a number of these scenarios, a less complicated structure exists that is easier to understand. The nested *If* block can be replaced with a standard If block that uses a logical operator. Generic and specific examples would be:

```
If cond1 And cond2 Then
        takeAction1
End If
```

would become . . .
```
If numHours > 40 And UCase(strDayType = "H" Then
        Let numRate = numRate * 2
End If
```

So far, we have seen a selection between two alternatives: either a choice between one of two separate actions, or a choice of either taking an action or taking no action. After the following exercises, you will be shown how to select the best alternative among *many* possible actions.

One final comment for those of you who have used GW Basic or QBasic languages for programming. Single-line statements were popular with earlier, unstructured versions of BASIC. Since one of the important goals of this text is to help you understand programming structures, single-line statements will not be used. Since your curiosity has now been aroused, the following is an example of the type of non-structured programming that will not be used in this text:

```
If cond Then takeAction1 Else takeAction2
```

It is difficult to determine what action is taking place as a result of this command. The use of structured programming helps make the program more understandable.

Exercise 6-2

1. Write a program to determine how much to tip the waiter in a fine restaurant. The tip should be 15 percent of the check, with a minimum of $1.
2. Write a quiz program to ask "Who was the first Ronald McDonald?" The program should display "Correct" if the answer is Willard Scott and otherwise should display "Nice try."
3. Write a program to handle a savings account withdrawal. The program should request the current balance and the amount of the withdrawal as input and then display the new balance. If the withdrawal is greater than the original balance, the program should display "Withdrawal denied." If the new balance is less than $150, the message "Balance below $150" should be displayed.

6-3.   IF/ELSE IF/END IF

You will encounter situations that require a choice among *many* alternatives, not just two. For those occasions, there are two programming constructs you may use. The first is presented in this section, the *If...ElseIf...End If* block, and the other in the next section, *Select Case*.

An *If...ElseIf...End If* block is used to present three or more alternatives for consideration, *only one of which may be selected and executed*. In general, an *If* block can contain any number of *ElseIf* statements; there is no upper limit. The general format for an If...ElseIf...End If block is:

```
If cond1 Then
        takeAction1
ElseIf cond2 Then
        takeAction2
```

```
ElseIf cond… Then        'Unlimited number of ElseIf statements
   takeAct…              'Action required for ElseIf statement
Else
   takeAct…
End If
```

When applied to our Gross Pay example, one application might be to determine which shift the employee worked, and therefore which shift differential should be applied to the employee's base rate of pay. The source code would be:

```
If strShift = "1" Then
    Let numShiftDiff = 0        'No bonus working a normal shift
ElseIf strShift = "2" Then
    Let numShiftDiff = .05
Else                           'If the employee does
    Let numShiftDiff = .10     'not work the 1st or 2nd shift,
                               he or she
End If                         'she must be working the 3rd
                               shift.
```

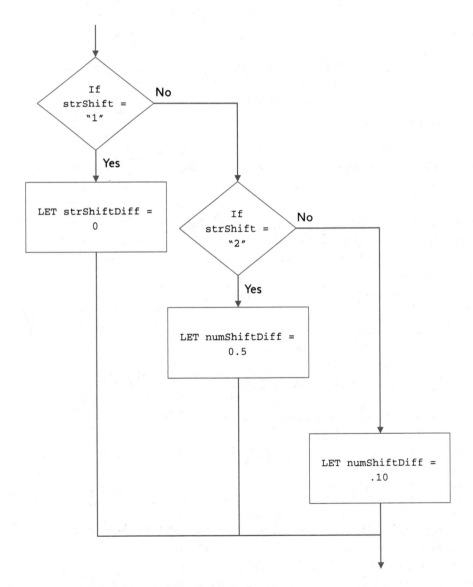

Figure 6-3. *If…ElseIf…End If* block example.

You are probably wondering what the flowchart for this example might look like. Your answer is shown in Figure 6-3. Note that the decision symbols are cascaded, indicating that the first condition is tested first, the second tested second, and so on. In fact, this is precisely the way the computer assesses each condition; one at a time, then if the condition is false, it moves to the next condition. You will also notice that there is no need for a third decision symbol for shift #3, the **Else** condition.

Notice also that no matter which option is selected, the program bypasses all other options within the *If...ElseIf...End If* block. In other words, program execution goes to the next statement immediately after the **End If** statement. Remember, regardless of how many options are available, *only one option will be selected and executed* among all the available options.

While the source code and flowchart from the previous example does not seem to be too complicated, it does get much more difficult to understand when there are a great number of options from which to choose. In these particular instances, the *Select Case* block, discussed in the next section, is a far better alternative.

■ Exercise 6-3

1. Federal law requires hourly employees be paid "time-and-a-half" for work in excess of 40 hours in a week. For example, if a person's hourly wage is $8 and he works 60 hours in a week, his gross pay should be

   $$(40 \times 8) + (1.5 \times 8 \times (60-40)) = \$560.$$

   Write a program that requests as input the number of hours a person works in a given week and his hourly wage, and then displays his gross pay.

2. The current calendar, called the Gregorian calendar, was introduced in 1582. Every year divisible by 4 was declared to be a leap year with the exception of the years ending in 00 (that is, those divisible by 100) and not divisible by 400. For instance, the years 1600 and 2000 are leap years, but 1700, 1800, and 1900 are not. Write a program that requests a year as input and states whether or not it is a leap year. (Test the program on the years 1994, 1995, 1900, and 2000.)

3. Write a program that allows the user 10 tries to answer the question "Which U.S. President was born on July 4?" After three incorrect guesses, the program should pop-up the hint, "He once said, 'If you don't say anything, you won't be called upon to repeat it' in a message box. After seven incorrect guesses, the program should give the hint, "His nickname was 'Silent Cal.' " The number of guesses should be displayed in a label. Note: Calvin Coolidge was born on July 4, 1872.

6-4.   SELECT CASE

A **Select Case block** is an efficient decision-making structure that simplifies choosing among several actions. It avoids complex nested *If* constructs. *If* blocks make decisions based on whether the condition evaluates as True or False. *Select Case* choices are determined by the value of an expression called the **selector**. The block is started with the expression **Select Case variable**, then each of the possible actions is given as **Case selector**. The following source code is based on the shift differential scenario from the Gross Pay example in the previous section. The string variable is *strShift* and the selectors are the string constants *"1"*, *"2"*, and *"3"*, in this example.

```
Select Case strShift
      Case "1"
            Let numShiftDiff = 0
      Case "2"
            Let numShift   Diff = .05
      Case Else
            Let numShiftDiff = .10
End Select
```

Select Case blocks are very flexible. They can be customized to meet a number of programming needs and scenarios. First, the *Case Else* statement is not required. You could have substituted **Case "3"** for the **Case Else** statement in the previous example, and the program would have worked fine. However, the *Case Else* statement is best employed as an *error check*. What if the user mistyped and entered a "4"? The new use for *Case Else*, shown below, would have dealt with the errant entry.

```
Select Case strShift
      Case "1"
            Let numShiftDiff = 0
      Case "2"
            Let numShiftDiff = .05
      Case "3"
            Let numShiftDiff = .10
      Case Else
            Picture1.Print "That is an invalid shift."
End Select
```

The *Case* can be multiple values separated by a comma, as in:

```
Case "1", "2"
```

This means that only these two values ("1" and "2") will cause the action statement to execute.

Case can also be an *inclusive range of values* such as 1, 2, 3, and 4:

```
Case 1 To 4
```

Case can involve a relational operator (which requires the **Is**), such as:

```
Case Is > 3
```

Although you will not use the next example, Case can be another variable, which is one of the ways to make your program ultimately flexible. That statement would appear as:

```
Case numVar            or...            Case strVar
```

With the introduction of variables, Case can also be an expression such as:

```
Case numShiftDiff + numRate
```

However, to maintain clarity and the principle of structured programming, we will be using only string constants or numeric constants as *selectors* in *Case* statements. Also, as you might expect, the flowchart has changed dramatically. Figure 6-4 shows the proper flowcharting technique for the *Select Case* programming construct.

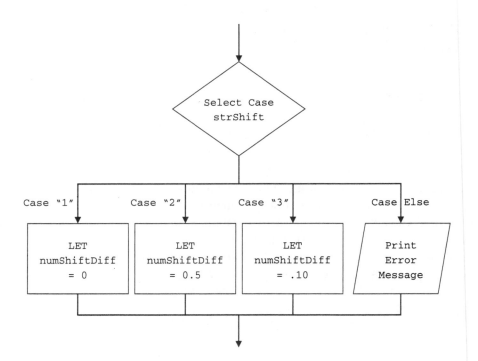

Figure 6-4. If / ElseIf / End If block example.

In every example, once the selector has determined which action will be taken, program execution continues with the next line immediately following the *End Select* statement. The other options are totally ignored.

Like *If* blocks, *Select Case* block statements do not have to be indented. For the purposes of this text, all source code for *If* blocks and *Select Case* blocks will be indented to maintain good structured programming. It is also very easy for you to locate the words *Select Case*, and scan down the block to find the *End Select* statement. You immediately know the variable being used and the number of different cases under consideration.

It is time to update our Gross Pay example using the programming constructs from this chapter. Note the changes in the user interface, Figure 6-5. One text box was added to indicate whether or not to deduct union dues, and a second text box to let the user indicate the shift worked. The source code for our Gross Pay example, with an *If* and a *Select Case* blocks inserted, is shown in Figure 6-6, and the now quite complicated flowchart in Figure 6-7.

As a final note for this section, every *If* block can be replaced with a *Select Case* block, and vice versa. A *Select Case* block is preferred over an *If* block when the possible choices have more or less the same importance.

So far, you have covered *Sequence* and *Selection*. After you complete the exercises in this section, we will begin *Iteration*, or looping.

Exercise 6-4

1. Suppose the selector of a Select Case block is the numeric variable *num*. Determine whether each of the following Case clauses is valid.

    (a) Case 1, 4, Is < 10

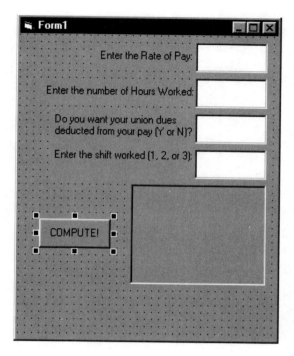

Figure 6-5. Revised Gross Pay user interface.

   (b) Case Is < 5, Is >= 5

   (c) Case num = 2

2. Do the following two programs always produce the same output for a whole number grade from 0 to 100?

```
grade = Val (txtBox.Text)        grade = Val (txtflox.Text)
Select Case grade                Select Case grade
  Case Is >= 90                  Case Is >= 90
     Picture1.Print "A."            Picture1.Print "1A"
  Case Is >= 60                  Case 60 To 89
     Picture1.Print "Pass"          Picture1.Print "Pass"
  Case Else                      Case 0 To 59
     Picture1.Print "Fail"          Picture1.Print "Fail"
End Select                       End Select
```

3. Table 5.4 shows the location of books in the library stacks according to their call numbers. Write a program that requests the call number of a book as input and displays the location of the book.

Call Numbers	Location
100 to 199	basement
200 to 500 and over 900	main floor
501 to 900 except 700 to 750	upper floor
700 to 750	archives

Table 5.4 Location of library books

4. Write a program that requests an exam score and assigns a letter grade with the scale 90–100 (A), 80–89 (B), 70–79 (C), 60–69 (D), 0–59 (F).

CHAPTER 7

ITERATION

7-1.   Introduction

Iteration, or looping, is the third most important programming construct. It is used to repeat a sequence of statements a number of times. You have already dealt with a limited type of iteration in the Manny the Robot example used in Chapter 1-3. At first, Manny could only do individual commands such as Step and Turn. Then, you programmed it to execute Step2 and Turn3. As Manny repeated, or *iterated*, the Step command twice in Step2 and the Turn command three times in Turn3, you were in effect looping each of the commands; making the command repeat a number of times.

That is the logic behind iteration—repeating commands. Now the question becomes, "How many times is the loop executed?"

Again, we borrow from things you have already learned. When studying Problem Solving Tools in Chapter 2, you learned that relational and logical operators are used to create a *condition* that will evaluate as True or False. In the same manner, a **Do...Loop** repeats a sequence of statements as long as a certain condition is True, or until that condition becomes True. You will get to see an example of how conditions are used in conjunction with loops in the next section.

In addition to repeating commands, we will use statements inside the loop to change the value of variables used within the loop. There are two special types of variables used in looping. A **counter** counts the number of times the loop executes, or repeats. To do this, the counter is usually **incremented** (increased) by +1 every time the commands in the loop are repeated.

The second special type of variable, an **accumulator**, is used to keep a running total. In other words, it *accumulates*, or adds, the variables' values as the program is looped. The counter is actually a special type of accumulator, but we prefer to keep the two separate. The counter records the number of times the loop is executed, and the accumulator keeps a running total of a variable's value. Let's take a closer look at loops and looping.

7-2.   DO...LOOP Loops

As previously stated, a **Do...Loop** repeats a sequence of statements as long as a certain condition is True, or until that condition becomes True. A **Do** statement begins the sequence of statements, and a **Loop** statement completes the sequence of statements.

For every *Do* there must be a corresponding *Loop*, and either the word *While* or *Until* must follow the word *Do* or the word *Loop*. The test condition appears either after *While* or after *Until*. Put all this together, and the four permissible **Do...Loop** structures are:

(1.) **Do While** condition is True

    Processing step 1

    Processing step 2

    Proc... etc.

Loop

(2.) **Do Until** condition becomes True

    Processing step 1

    Processing step 2

    Proc... etc.

Loop

(3.) **Do**

    Processing step 1

    Processing step 2

    Proc... etc.

Loop While condition is True

(4.) **Do**

    Processing step 1

    Processing step 2

    Proc... etc.

Loop Until condition becomes True

Even though all four are correct, for the sake of simplicity, we will only be using numbers 1 and 4, the *Do While...Loop* and *Do...Loop Until* structures. We do this because:

- Any While statement can be easily converted to an Until statement and vice versa.

- This restriction produces no loss of capability.

- The programmer has two fewer structures to worry about.

- The word While is associated with testing at the top of the loop, and the word Until is associated with testing at the bottom of the loop.

- Certain other structured languages, such as Pascal, allow While only at the top of the loop and Until at the bottom.

- The convention simplifies reading and deskchecking a program.

The phrase **test condition** has been used several times. It literally means to check the truth value of the condition. Since a **Do While** statement is tested at the top of the loop, the statements inside the loop may or may not be executed. If the **Do While** condition evaluates as True, all statements within the loop are executed. When the program reaches the **Loop** statement, program execution returns to the **Do** statement and the **Do While** condition is tested once again. This iteration will continue as long as the **Do While** condition evaluates True.

If the **Do While** condition evaluates False, none of the statements in the loop will be executed. The entire **Do...Loop** structure is skipped, and execution continues with the statement immediately following the **Loop** statement. Figure 7-1 shows the flowchart for a **Do While** loop that is used in our Gross Pay example. If there are 10 employees being paid, the commands to calculate their gross pay will repeat ten times (when Count = 0, 1, 2, 3, 4, 5, 6, 7, 8, and 9).

If the test condition is evaluated using a **Loop Until** statement, all the statements within the loop will execute at least once. This happens because there is no test condition at the **Do** statement to prevent the program from entering the loop and executing statements within the loop. The test condition will not be evaluated until the end of the loop, i.e. the truth value is evaluated last.

If the **Loop Until** condition is True, execution of the loop will cease, and the next statement after the **Loop Until** will be executed. If the **Loop Until** condition is False, execution returns to the **Do** statement, and all statements within the loop will be executed until the **Loop Until** condition evaluates True. Figure 7-2 shows a flowchart using the Gross Pay example for 10 employees.

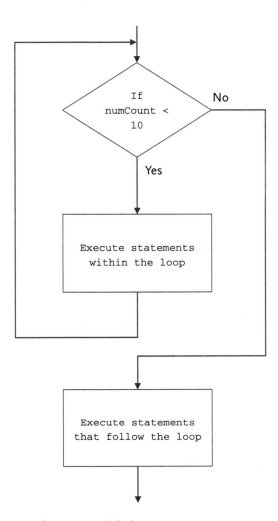

Figure 7-1. Flowchart for a *Do While* loop.

If you were to create source code that would display the numbers from 1 to 10, the code for the **Do While** and **Loop Until** structures would be like that in Figures 7-3 and 7-4.

Both examples will display the numbers 1 to 10, but note the difference in the conditions. Deskcheck each until you are comfortable with the reasons why each is so different from the other. You will find that converting **Do While...Loop** conditions to **Do...Loop Until** conditions requires that you change the relational operator to the exact opposite relationship. In other words, = becomes <>, > becomes <=, < becomes >=, and so on.

However, when constructing loops, you must try to avoid the infinite loop—that is loops that are never exited. An **infinite loop** occurs when the condition is always true. For example, if you used the Loop Until condition of numNumber >0, the loop will continue to execute into infinity since you assigned the value 1 to numNumber before the loop started. Incrementing numNumber by +1 means that it will always be greater than 0, hence an infinite or continuous loop.

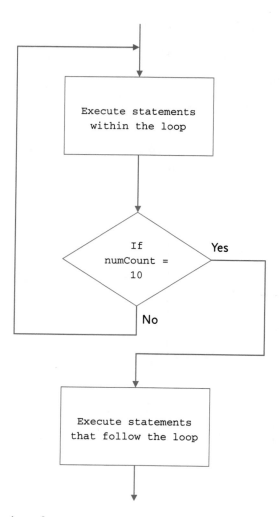

Figure 7-2. Flowchart for a *Loop Until* loop.

As with the other programming constructs you have encountered, Do…Loop statements do not have to be indented. However, for the sake of clarity of programming and good structured programming practice, please using indenting in all your programs, especially when creating a loop.

It is always a good idea to assign a value to all variables to be used within a loop. This gives you a known starting place for the value of all your variables, which may help you debug your program later.

When using a Do…Loop in conjunction with an external data file (Chapter 5-2), you may want to put an **EOD** flag in the data to indicate End Of Data. That way, you can control the loop by using source code similar to that in Figure 7-5.

A word of caution. If you are reading the strName, numHours, and num-Rate, then you must also provide data for the other variables. That means that the last series of data in the file must be **"EOD", 0, 0** to assign "EOD" to str-Name, the first 0 to numHours, and the second 0 to numRate.

Just as we nested IF statements, we can also nest loops. This is when indenting really pays off, for it is easy to see when you do or do not have a **Loop** for

```
Project1 - Form1 (Code)
Command1                          Click
    Private Sub Command1_Click()
        'Display the numbers from 1 to 10
        Picture1.Cls
        Let numNumber = 1
        Do While numNumber < 11
            Picture1.Print numNumber
            Let numNumber = numNumber + 1
        Loop
    End Sub
```

Figure 7-3. Program example of a *Do While...Loop* loop.

```
Project1 - Form1 (Code)
Command1                          Click
    Private Sub Command1_Click()
        'Display the numbers from 1 to 10
        Picture1.Cls
        Let numNumber = 1
        Do
            Picture1.Print numNumber
            Let numNumber = numNumber + 1
        Loop Until numNumber = 11
    End Sub
```

Figure 7-4. Programming example of a *Do...Loop Until* loop.

```
Project1 - Form1 (Code)
Command1                          Click
    Private Sub Command1_Click()
        'Read data from an external file
        Picture1.Cls
        Open "C:\WINDOWS\PAYDATA.TXT" For Input As #1
        Do While strName <> "EOD"
            Input #1, strName
        Loop
        Close #1
    End Sub
```

Figure 7-5. Using a *Do While...Loop* to process data from an external file.

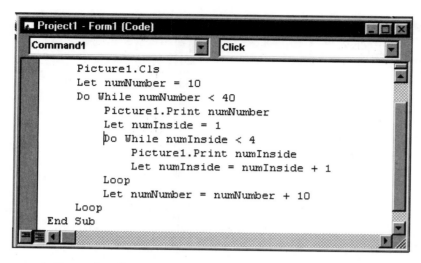

```
Project1 - Form1 (Code)

Command1                    Click

        Picture1.Cls
        Let numNumber = 10
        Do While numNumber < 40
            Picture1.Print numNumber
            Let numInside = 1
            Do While numInside < 4
                Picture1.Print numInside
                Let numInside = numInside + 1
            Loop
            Let numNumber = numNumber + 10
        Loop
    End Sub
```

Figure 7-6. Example of nested *Do...Loop*s.

every **Do**. Figure 7-6 is an example of nested loops. What will be displayed in the picture box after this program has been executed?

Not fair! You already looked at Figure 7-7 below! If you did not come up with the correct answer, you may want to "play computer" and deskcheck the code until you come up with the same output as in Figure 7-7. Then again, you may wish to move on before you get too severe a headache. In either case, you will not be given problems with nested loops in this text. What your professor decides to do is another situation entirely.

Next we will explore a special type of looping construct, the *For...Next* loop.

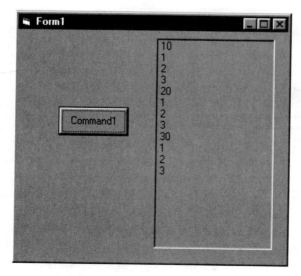

Figure 7-7. Answer to nested *Do...Loop* example.

■ **Exercise 7-2**

1. Write a program that displays a Celsius-to=Fahrenheit conversion table. Entries in the table should range from −40 to 40 degrees Celsius in increments of 5 degrees. *Note:* The formula $f = (9/5) * c + 32$ converts Celsius to Fahrenheit.

In Exercises 2 through 3, write a program to solve the stated problem.

2. *Savings Account.* $15,000 is deposited into a savings account paying 5 percent interest and $1000 is withdrawn from the account at the end of each year. Approximately how many years are required for the savings account to be depleted? (*Note:* If at the end of a certain year the balance is $1000 or less, then the final withdrawal will consist of that balance and the account will be depleted.)

3. $1000 is deposited into a savings account, and an additional $1000 is deposited at the end of each year. If the money earns interest at the rate of 5 percent, how long will it take before the account contains at least $1 million?

7-3. FOR...NEXT Loops

A **FOR...NEXT** loop is used when we know exactly how many times a loop should be executed. It is a special looping structure that is easy to read, easy to write, and has features that make it ideal for certain common tasks. The basic form of the command is:

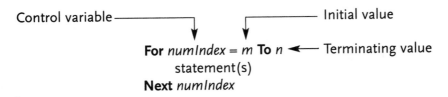

The **For** statement uses a **control variable** (numIndex) to control the looping which will execute a specific number of times, that being from the **initial value** (m) to the **terminating value** (n). It is assumed that the initial value is less than the terminating value, and that it will be incremented by +1 every time the **Next** statement is executed. The **Next** statement also returns control of the loop back to the **For** statement where the control variable is once again tested. After the terminating value has been exceeded, execution continues with the statement immediately following the **Next** statement.

For a precise example, assume that you want the loop to execute three times, from *numIndex* = 1 to *numIndex* = 3. Execution will be as follows:

1. The **For** statement will assign the value 1 to *numIndex* as the loop begins to execute. Program statements within the loop are executed for the first time. The **Next** statement is executed, which causes *numIndex* to be incremented by +1 to 2. Program execution returns to the **For** statement where the value of *numIndex* (2) is tested to see if it exceeds the terminal value (3), which it does not.

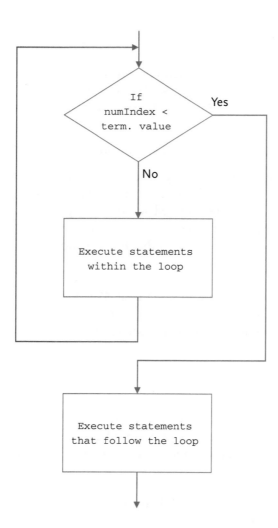

Figure 7-8. Flowchart for a *For...Next* loop.

2. The loop is executed a second time. When the **Next** statement is reached, *numIndex* is incremented by +1 from 2 to 3. Execution is returned to the **For** statement where *numIndex* is tested to see if it exceeds the terminal value of 3. In this instance, *numIndex* equals the terminal value but <u>does not exceed it</u>, so the loop will execute a third time.

3. The **Next** statement increments *numIndex* to 4, execution passes back to the For statement where *numIndex* is tested for the last time. Now 4 exceeds 3, the looping is stopped, and execution continues with the statement immediately following the **Next** statement.

The flowchart for a **For...Next** loop would look like Figure 7-8.

The control variable can be any numeric variable. The most common names are *numIndex* and *numVal*. If possible, the name should suggest the purpose of the control variable.

The initial and terminating values can be constants, variables, or expressions. For instance, you could assign a value to the initial and terminating values before the loop, then use those variables. An example would be:

```
Let numStartYr = 1960
Let numEndYr = 1999
For numIndex = numStartYr To numEndYr
        Statement(s)
Next numIndex
```

You could even ask the user to enter the values for numStartYr and numEndYr with the caution that numStartYr must be a lower number than numEndYr.

Using our ever-popular Gross Pay example, the source code for a For...Next loop appears like that in Figure 7-9.

On occasion, you may need to increment the control variable by more than +1, or you may need to use a terminal value that is less than the initial value (*n* is less than *m*). The **For...Next** looping structure can accommodate both scenarios through the use of the **Step** command. The traditional layout for a **Step** command is:

```
For numIndex = m To n Step s
```

Substituting numeric values for *m*, *n*, and *s*, a short example would be:

```
For numIndex = 1 To 6 Step 2
        Picture1.Print numIndex
Next numIndex
```

On the first pass, *numIndex* = 1, and 1 is printed. At the **Next** statement, *numIndex* is incremented by +2 making its value 3. *numIndex* is tested at the **For** statement, and 3 is printed. *numIndex* is incremented by +2 to 5 at the **Next** statement, then tested at the **For** statement. 5 is printed and *numIndex* is incremented at the **Next** statement again by +2, making the value 7. When tested at the **For** statement, *numIndex* exceeds the terminal value of 6, looping ceases, and execution is passed to the statement immediately after the **Next** statement.

Step can be used to decrement the control variable. For instance, the **For...Next** loop may appear as follows:

```
For numIndex = 5 To 1 Step - 3
        Picture1.Print numIndex
Next numIndex
```

```
Project1 - Form1 (Code)                              _ □ ✕
Command1                    ▼   Click                       ▼

    Private Sub Command1_Click()
        Picture1.Cls
        For numIndex = 1 To 10        'Ten employees to be paid
            Let strName = InputBox("Enter employee name")
            Let numRate = InputBox("Enter rate of pay")
            Let numHours = InputBox("Enter hours worked")
            Let numGrossPay = numRate * numHours
            Picture1.Print strName, numGrossPay
        Next numIndex
    End Sub
```

Figure 7-9. Source code for a *For...Next* loop.

In this case, *numIndex* is equal to 5, and 5 would be printed. At the **Next** statement, *numIndex* is decremented by -3, so the value would be 2. When tested at the **For** statement, 2 is greater than the terminal value 1, so statements within the loop are executed again. 2 is printed, *numIndex* is decremented by -3 to -1. Now, when tested at the **For** statement, -1 is less than the terminal value, so looping stops and execution goes to the statement immediately after the **Next** statement. Using a decrement reverses the Step logic, i.e. you are looking for a control variable value that is <u>less than</u> the terminal value, not one that is greater than the terminal value as in normal incrementing.

Just as we could nest **If...ElseIf...End If** and **Do...Loop** statements, we can also nest **For...Next** statements. As with both of the foregoing, it is most important to keep your logic straight. Nothing helps more than proper indentation of source code!

Another hint would be to make sure that the control variable is not adjusted in any way by statements within the loop. To do so may cause an infinite loop or other programming problems.

▪ Exercise 7-3

1. Suppose $800 is deposited into a savings account earning 4 percent interest compounded annually, and $100 is added to the account at the end of each year. Calculate the amount of money in the account at the end of 10 years. (Determine a formula for computing the balance at the end of 1 year based on the balance at the beginning of the year. Then write a program that starts with a balance of $800 and makes 10 passes through a loop containing the formula to produce the final answer.)

2. A TV set is purchased with a loan of $563 to be paid off with five monthly payments of $116. The interest rate is 1 percent per month. Display a table giving the balance on the loan at the end of each month.

3. Write a program to estimate how much a young worker will make before retiring at age 65. Request the worker's name, age, and starting salary as input. Assume the worker receives a 5 percent raise each year. For example, if the user enters Helen, 25, and 20000, then the picture box should display the following:

    Helen will earn about $2,415,995.25

7-4.   WHILE...WEND Loops

As you examine programs in your workplace or in other texts, you may encounter another looping structure that was used over a decade ago. This structure is called the *While...Wend* loop. The **While...Wend** loop is a carry-over from GW Basic, and is used in exactly the same manner as a **Do...Loop** would be used. For example, a typical **While...Wend** loop would appear as follows:

```
Let numEmployee = 1
While numEmployee < 11
    Picture1.Print numEmployee
    Let numEmployee = numEmployee + 1
Wend
```

As you can see, there are a number of similarities between the two types of loop structures. Both request that the value for variables used in the loop be assigned before entering the loop structure. They both employ the test While, which is executed at the start of the loop. My only purpose in bringing this to you is so you can better understand older programs you may see on your job. Normally, you will be using either the **Do...Loop** or **For...Next** looping structures.

Exercise 7-4

Convert the **Do...Loop** programs you did in Section 7-2 to **While...Wend** loops.

CHAPTER 8

ARRAYS

8-1 Introduction

In every assignment up to this point, you have been using **simple variables;** numeric and string variables that can hold only one value at a time. For instance, when you were processing the gross pay for the first employee, the variables used (i.e. *strName, numRate,* and *numHours*) retained the values that applied to that particular employee. When the data for the second employee was entered, it replaced the data of the first employee. There was no way to reclaim the first employee's data either for verification or for further processing. However, there is a programming construct that will retain the data for further use. This structure is called an *array*.

An array is unique in many ways. An **array** stores several values for the same variable, but in multiple locations in the computer's memory. In many business applications, arrays have been called *tables* or *lists,* as in a table or list of state abbreviations.

In any case, an **array variable** is used to indicate that the data being stored have commonality among them. An array variable is often referred to as a **subscripted variable,** a term that comes from mathematics, where subscripts are used to designate multiple values of a common variable. It is the subscript which distinguishes a simple variable from an array variable. The standard format for an array variable is:

```
numVariable(n)          OR          strVariable(n)
```

where the subscript includes the parenthesis and a numeric value, *n*. Simple variables do not have a subscript, so it is easy to distinguish between the two.

Arrays are either *static* or *dynamic.* A **static array** will not change during the execution of a program. The number of memory locations being reserved stays the same as well as the name of the array variable being used to access them. The next section presents the three types of arrays (simple, two-dimensional, and parallel) as static arrays; arrays that remain the same size once they have been dimensioned.

A **dynamic array** requires special actions. First, the programmer must designate the number of array locations as a variable, i.e. **strElmSt**(*numVar*). Secondly, the programmer must use a special type of dimensioning statement, the **ReDim** statement, to allow an open-ended value for the last element of the array. Finally, a statement, or statements, must be placed in the program that allows the user to determine the size of the array by providing a value for *numVar.* A dynamic array is much more flexible, and can even be changed during program execution. The last section of this chapter deals with the techniques of programming dynamic arrays, an approach that can be used in all three (simple, two-dimensional, and parallel) configurations.

The final section deals with one of the most popular applications of arrays, the **bubble sort.**

8-2. Static Arrays

Once again, a **static array** will not change during the execution of a program.

Simple Arrays. **A simple array** is a lot like a row of mail boxes for houses located on a specific street. The example would be as follows:

	(1)	(2)	(3)	(4)	(5)
strElmSt( )					

Using this scenario, mail for people who live in 1 Elm Street would be placed into the box (array location) **strElmSt(1)**—read as "Elm Street sub 1." **strElmSt** is the name of the string array, and (1) is the first location in that array. There may be no mail for *strElmSt(2)* or *strElmSt(3),* in which case their default value would be *null*. **Null** is a term that means no string value, or nothing. It is unlike zero, for 0 is a real number on a number line. Null has no value whatsoever.

Normally, a programmer tells the computer how many memory locations to reserve for the array. This process is referred to as **dimensioning the array.** The number of memory locations must be equal to or greater than the number of values stored for the array variable. If it is less, an error message will be displayed.

You use the **Dim** statement to dimension an array. Typical **Dim** statements for a simple numeric or a simple string array would be:

```
Dim strStudent(1 To 30) As String
        OR
Dim numScore(1 To 30) As Integer
```

In either case, the statement reserves registers in RAM with the temporary labels of *strStudent(1)* through *strStudent(30)*, or *numScore(1)* through *numScore(30)*. The first number indicates both the number (subscript) of the first element and the beginning of the array, and the second number indicates both the number of the last element and the end of the array. It would also be possible to have 30 elements in the strStudent( ) array by using the dimension statement:

```
Dim strStudent(31 To 60) As String
```

Now, the first element would be *strStudent(31)* and the last element *strStudent(60),* with a total of 30 elements in the array. You do not have to start your array at 1, but it is often easiest to track the data using 1 as the first element.

Values can be assigned to subscripted variables with assignment statements, and can be displayed with Print methods. For instance, consider the following program segment:

```
Dim numScore(1 To 4) As Integer
Picture1.Cls
Let numScore(1) = 87
Let numScore(3) = 92
For numIndex = 1 To 4
        Picture1.Print numScore(numIndex)
Next numIndex
```

When the program is run, the printout is 87 0 92 0 . Therefore, a value is retained for both numScore(1) and numScore(3), and the default value of zero for any numeric variable, subscripted or not, is also printed. A more visual representation of memory allocations would be:

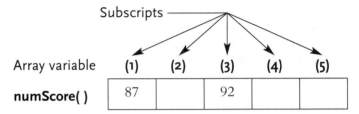

On occasion, you may hear the subscripted variable referred to as an element. The name of the element, or location, has the same two parts: the array name and the subscript.

Two-dimensional Arrays. Each array discussed so far was dimensioned to accommodate a single list of items. Such array variables are called single-subscripted variables. An array can also be dimensioned to accommodate the contents of a table with several rows and columns. Such arrays are called **two-dimensional arrays**, and they use **double-subscripted variables**. The format for dimensioning these arrays is:

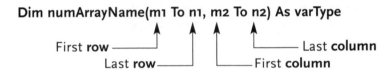

Note that the two subscripts deal with the number of rows, then with the number of columns. All data in the table will share the same array variable. This concept is illustrated by Figure 8-1, a table that gives the road mileage between U. S. cities. It uses three rows and four columns for the data, and the double-subscripted array variables indicate the row and column of that specific piece of data.

	Chicago	Los Angeles	New York	Philadelphia
Chicago	0	2054	802	738
Los Angeles	2054	0	2786	2706
New York	802	2786	0	100

Figure 8-1. Road mileage between U.S. cities.

The dimensioning statement for Figure 8-1 would be:

```
Dim numDist(1 To 3, 1 To 5) as Integer
```

Therefore, the designation of each double-subscripted variable and its value would be:

numDist(1,1)=0   numDist(1,2)=2054   numDist(1,3)=802   numDist(1,4)=738
numDist(2,1)=2054   numDist(2,2)=0   numDist(2,3)=2786   numDist(2,4)=2706
numDist(3,1)=802   numDist(3,2)=2786   numDist(3,3)=0   numDist(3,4)=100

Using Figure 8-1, the first double-subscripted variable, *numDist(1,1)*, gives the value for row 1, column 2, or 0. The value for the second double-subscripted variable, *numDist(1,2)*, can be found in row 1, column 2, or 2054.

Parallel Arrays. **Parallel arrays** consist of two or more individual arrays, dimensioned the same size, that do not use the same variable name, but they do have something in common between them. For example, in our Gross Pay example, *strName( )*, *numRate( )*, and *numHours( )* all pertain to the same employee. Therefore, they share a commonality, that of being used to calculate the gross pay for that particular employee. They can be dimensioned as follows:

```
Dim strName(1 To 100) As String
Dim numRate(1 To 100) As Integer
Dim numHours(1 To 100) As Integer
```

This means that the first employee's name would be in *strName(1)*, his or her rate of pay in *numRate(1)*, and the number of hours he or she worked in *numHours(1)*. Employee number 2's data would be in *strName(2)*, *numRate(2)*, *numHours(2)*, and so on with the rest of the employees.

Regardless of whether the array is a simple array, a two-dimensional array, or a parallel array, the purpose is the same; to store values for use later in the program. Up to now, they have also shared the characteristic of being dimensioned ahead of time, according to the wishes of the programmer.

However, predetermined dimensioning has limited applicability. The programmer would have to know well ahead of time the largest number of elements needed throughout the life of the program. This is nearly impossible. To solve this problem of a lack of flexibility, *dynamic arrays*—the subject of the next section—were created.

Exercise 8-2

In exercises 1 and 2, determine the output displayed in the picture box when the command button is clicked. All **Dim** statements for arrays are in the *General Declarations* section.

1. Dim a(1 To 20) As Integer

```
Private Sub Command1_Click()
    Let a(5) = 1
    Let a(10) = 2
    Let numAns = a(5) + a(10)
    Picture1.Print numAns
End Sub
```

2. Dim a(1 To 20, 1 To 30) As Single

```
Private Sub Command1_Click()
    Let a(3, 5) = 6
    Let a(5, 3) = 2 * a(3, 5)
    Picture1.Print a(5, 3)
End Sub
```

3. Given the following flight schedule,

Flight	Origin	Destination	Departure Time
117	Tucson	Dallas	8:45 a.m.
239	Boston	Los Angeles	10:15 a.m.
298	Albany	Las Vegas	1:35 p.m.
326	St. Paul	New York	2:40 p.m.
445	St. Louis	Tampa	4:20 p.m.

write a program to load this information into four arrays of range 1 to 5, *strFlight(), strOrig(), strDest(),* and *strTime(),* and ask the user to request a flight number. Have the computer find the flight number and display the information corresponding to that flight. Account for the case where a user requests a nonexistent flight.

4. Dimension the string array Stooges() with subscripts ranging from 1 to 3. Assign the three values Moe, Larry, and Curly to the array as soon as the command button is clicked. Display each stooge name, one at a time, letting the user make a comment about the stooge before moving to the next one. Record the user's comments and print out the three stooges and the comments made by the user.

8-3.   Dynamic Arrays

In actual practice, the amount of data that a program will need to store is often not known in advance. Programs should be flexible and incorporate a method for handling varying amounts of data. This is accomplished by using a two-step dimensioning technique. The first involves the use of a special dimensioning statement, the **ReDim** statement. Secondly, a variable must be used for the end value in the dimensioning statement, the value of which will be provided by the user later during program execution, and before the array is used. An array whose range has been specified by a ReDim statement is referred to as a dynamic array. This feature was added with the release of Visual Basic 6.0.

A typical ReDim statement would be:

```
ReDim arrayName(1 To numVar) As varType
```

At a designated point in the program, the user is asked to provide a value for *numVar*. This technique can be used in simple arrays, two-dimensional arrays, or parallel arrays as the following three examples illustrate:

```
        (Simple array) ReDim strName(1 to numVar) As String

 (Two-dimensional array) ReDim strName(1 to numRow, 1 To numCol) As
                         String

        (Parallel array) ReDim strName(1 To numVar) As String
                         ReDim numRate(1 To numVar) As Integer
                         ReDim numHours(1 To numVar) As Integer
```

In each instance, the arrays have been made more responsive to the user's need, and the programming made more flexible with perhaps a longer useful life in the application.

■ Exercise 8-3

Create a program that will tell the user both the total of deposits they made to their savings this year, and the average deposit. Since you will not know how many deposits they made, you will have to prompt the user to enter the total number of deposits made in the last year. After that, you must store the values for each deposit as they are entered so you can use them later in your calculations.

8-4.   Bubble Sort

A **sort** is an algorithm for ordering an array. Of the many different techniques for sorting an array, one is presented as an example of the utility of arrays.

The **bubble sort** is an algorithm that compares adjacent items and swaps those that are out of order. If this process is repeated enough times, the list will be ordered. Let's carry out this process, for a list of employees: Joe, Ron, Lois, and Bud. The steps for each pass through the list are as follows:

1. Compare the first and second items. If they are out of order, swap them.

2. Compare the second and third items. If they are out of order, swap them.

3. Repeat this pattern for all remaining pairs. The final comparison and possible swap are between the second-to-last and last elements.

The first time through the list, this process is repeated to the end of the list. This is called the first pass. After the first pass, the last item (Ron) will be in its proper position. Therefore, the second pass does not have to consider it and so requires one less comparison. At the end of the second pass, the last two items will be in their proper position. (Items in Figure 8-2 that have reached their proper position have been <u>underlined</u>.) Each successive pass requires one less comparison. After four passes, the last four items will be in their proper positions, and hence, the first will be also. Note that on the last two passes, no physical rearrangement was needed, but the comparison verified the correct location.

The program that will accomplish this complex task requires the use of a pair of nested loops, as shown in Figure 8-3. The inner loop performs a single pass, and the outer loop controls the number of passes.

When using the bubble sort, you may find it advantageous to use the **UCase** function, since **RON** has a different value than **Ron**. The uppercase **RON** will be placed at the top of the list, ahead of Bud, since uppercase letters are of a lower ASCII value than are lower case letters.

UCase is also used to prevent user entry errors. In this way, all data is in upper case and therefore equal during searching and sorting.

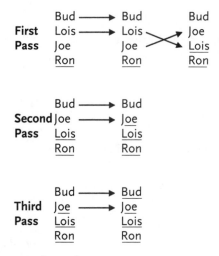

Figure 8-2. Bubble sort of employees.

```
Private Sub Command1_Click()
    'Bubble sort program to produce an ordered list of employees
    Dim strName(1 To 4) As String          'Employee names
    Dim numPass As Integer                  'Number of passes
    Dim numIndex As Integer
    Dim strTemp As String
    'Load the employee array
    Let strName(1) = "Lois"
    Let strName(2) = "Bud"
    Let strName(3) = "Ron"
    Let strName(4) = "Joe"
    'Begin bubble sort
    For numPass = 1 To 3                    '1 less pass than data items
        For numIndex = 1 To 4 - numPass    '1 less comparison per pass
            If strName(numIndex) > strName(numIndex + 1) Then
                Let strTemp = strName(numIndex)
                Let strName(numIndex) = strName(numIndex + 1)
                Let strName(numIndex + 1) = strTemp
            End If
        Next numIndex
    Next numPass
    'Print out the final ordered employee list
    Picture1.Cls
    For numIndx = 1 To 4
        Picture1.Print strName(numIndx)
    Next numIndx
```

Figure 8-3. Bubble sort program.

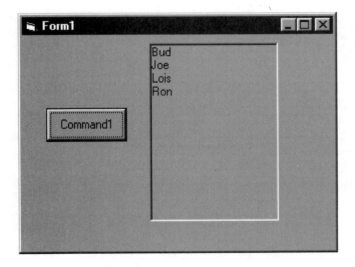

Figure 8-4. Results of the bubble sort of employees.

After the program in Figure 8-3 is run, the output looks like that in Figure 8-4.

Exercise 8-4

Display the names of the seven dwarfs in alphabetical order. In case you have forgotten who they were, the data you will use are:

Doc, Grumpy, Sleepy, Happy, Bashful, Sneezy, Dopey

CHAPTER 9

SUBROUTINES

9-1. Introduction

Large problems usually require large programs. One method programmers use to make a large problem more understandable is to divide it into smaller, less complex sub-problems. Known as the *"divide-and-conquer"* or **stepwise refinement** approach, this methodology is the heart of top-down, modular design.

The greatest advantage to modular programming is that it promotes structured programming. Beginning with the purpose of the program, subprograms are created that break down a problem into individual tasks, or modules. The modules and their relationship are presented first in a *hierarchy chart*, and eventually into a more detailed set of flowcharts. As stepwise refinement continues, complex modules are broken down even further if needed. An example of this process is the car loan, Figure 9-1.

While this is a good start, each of these tasks can be refined into more specific sub-tasks, as illustrated in Figure 9-2.

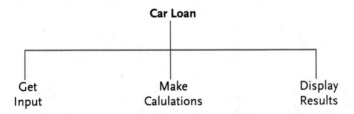

Figure 9-1. Beginning of a hierarchy chart for a car loan program.

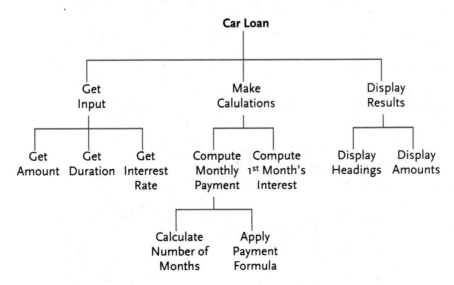

Figure 9-2. Final hierarchy chart for the car loan example.

Although there is no formal definition of the term structured programming, computer programmers are in uniform agreement that such programs should have a modular design and use only the three main types of programming structures mentioned earlier in this text: sequence, selection, and iteration.

The final chapter of this text is devoted to making these complex problems more manageable by making them easier to program and to debug. This is done by employing subroutines.

9-2. Establishing Subroutines and Stub Programming

A **subroutine** is a part of a program that performs one or more related tasks, has its own name, and is written as a separate part of the program. The programs you have been creating are actually subroutines of the Visual Basic program. However, you have treated the primary subroutine as the main program, which is exactly what you must do.

However, we will be creating and invoking subroutines that will be called by that main program. The simplest type of Sub procedure has the form of:

```
Private Sub ProcedureName()
      Statements(s)
End Sub
```

Subroutines are invoked, or called, with a **call statement** of the following form:

```
Call ProcedureName
```

As previously stated, complex problems often produce complex programs. It is quite easy to get lost in the changing screen, myriad variables, and multiple tasks. One technique to help develop and debug the program is to use *stub programming*. In this technique, the key event routines, and perhaps some smaller subroutines, are coded first. Temporary dummy procedures, or *stubs*, are written for the remaining subroutines. A stub procedure might consist of a print statement that would indicate if and when the subroutine was called. The source code for the actual task would be substituted for the stub at a later time.

Stubs can also be used to check the assignment and passing of variables between subroutines. The stub is always simpler than the actual program, so you are less likely to lose track of the variables.

Putting these concepts together, you get a program with subroutines and stubs such as that in Figure 9-3. As you review Figure 9-3, let's walk through how the computer executes a program with subroutines.

1. As you know, **Private Sub Command1_Click()** is the start of the main program, and the **Picture1.Cls** statement clears the picture box of any residual output from other programs.

2. The next statement, Call InputIt, does two things. First, it checks to see if there is a subroutine named *InputIt*. Then, If the program contains a subroutine with that name, the computer invokes, or executes, that procedure, passing control to the *InputIt* subroutine.

3. **Sub InputIt()** is merely the non-executable title of that subroutine. Execution continues with the statement immediately following the subroutine title.

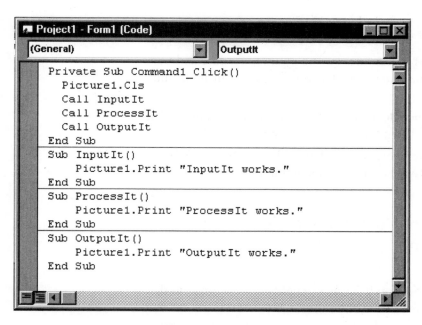

```
Project1 - Form1 (Code)                              _ □ ×
(General)                    ▼   OutputIt                ▼
    Private Sub Command1_Click()
       Picture1.Cls
       Call InputIt
       Call ProcessIt
       Call OutputIt
    End Sub
    Sub InputIt()
       Picture1.Print "InputIt works."
    End Sub
    Sub ProcessIt()
       Picture1.Print "ProcessIt works."
    End Sub
    Sub OutputIt()
       Picture1.Print "OutputIt works."
    End Sub
```

Figure 9-3. A program with subroutines and stubs.

4. The statement **Picture1.Print "InputIt works"** is a stub placed in the *InputIt* subroutine to indicate that it was successfully called into being, and that it works properly.

5. Once the quote has been output, the **End Sub** statement returns control to the main program, *to the statement immediately following the call statement that invoked that subroutine.*

6. Steps 2 through 5 are repeated for the *ProcessIt()* and *OutputIt()* subroutines, returning control to the main program every time the subroutine has completed its task.

7. Finally, the **End Sub** statement in the main program is encountered (the one immediately following *Call OutputIt*), which terminates program execution. The output for this stubbed procedure is at Figure 9-4.

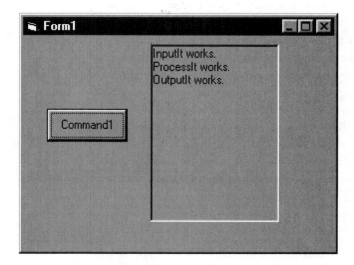

Figure 9-4. Output from the stub program in Figure 9-3.

Exercise 9-2

1. Create a program that uses subroutines for the input, processing and output. Substitute stubs for the statements that you would normally include within each subroutine.

2. Modify the program to include an IF...ELSE...END IF statement that calls different subroutines depending on some condition.

3. Modify the program once more and include a loop (DO...LOOP or FOR...NEXT) that displays the stub statement a number of times.

9-3.   General Declarations (Global Variables and Global Arrays)

The stub program presented in Section 9-2 was a straight-forward program that contained only output statements in the subroutines. However, there are few programs in business that require such simplistic output. Normal processing requires input, processing, and output. To accomplish these processes through subroutines requires the use of variables, which in turn mandates that these variables be declared either *global* or *local* variables. Local variables will be covered in the next section.

Global variables are shared throughout a program and are therefore eligible to be used anywhere in a program. This also means that regardless of whether the variable was in the main program or in one or more subroutines, the value of the variable can be changed in any of the modules. This attribute of global variables can be advantageous, and it can be very troublesome.

On the positive side, a global variable can be one value in the main, adjusted in a subroutine, and used in later statements in the main with the newly adjusted value. In addition, beginning programmers are usually more successful at getting programs to run in a shorter time using global variables. Finally, the process of declaring all variables at the beginning of a program helps provide the programmer a ready reference list of all variables in the program.

On the negative side, global variables—like all variables—must be spelled correctly every time they are used. It is easy to misspell a variable's name in a subroutine and not notice the error. (Hence the need to refer to that list of global variables declared at the beginning of the program.) It is also impossible to prevent the variable's value from being altered in another subroutine. Sharing means it is vulnerable to being changed. Lastly, when using a group of programmers to produce a subroutine each, combining their subprocedures becomes a nightmare. If you are unfortunate enough to have different spellings for the same variable in your program, the program will probably not work properly. Debugging misspelled variables can be very time consuming.

Variables can be added or removed from the *General Declarations* section any time during coding. This will have no adverse effect as long as the variable is spelled correctly (adding) or not used anywhere in the program (removing).

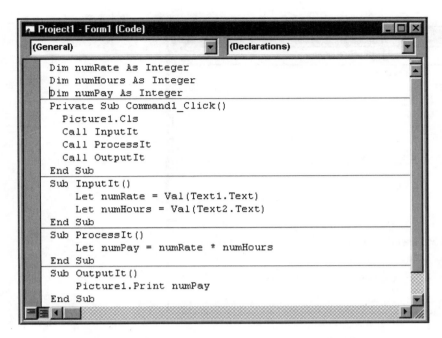

Figure 9-5. Global variables used in a program with subroutines.

Figure 9-5 illustrates the use of global variables in a program using subroutines. The variables are declared first in the *General Declarations* section, which is the section immediately above the first solid line.

Note that the cursor is in the *General Declarations* section, and that title appears in the Procedure window.

The program in Figure 9-5 is structured properly for each subroutine performs only one type of task. Variables are used correctly because their values are assigned/altered in only one procedure. The program makes the most efficient use of the "divide-and-conquer" methodology, for debugging the input is done in the *InputIt* subroutine, processing in the *ProcessIt* subprocedure, and so on.

Global Arrays

When an array is dimensioned in the *General Declarations* section, it and its values can be shared among the entire program in the same way that simple variables were shared. Consider Figure 9-6. The array for the scores is dimensioned before the program begins, making the *numScore()* array a global array. Therefore, the subroutines need only have an empty set of parenthesis to use the array. Note that the variable is also in the *General Declarations* section, and that arguments are not needed in the calling statements.

It is also important to note that, like simple variables, global subscripted variables can also be changed anywhere in the program. The use of good structured programming techniques can help prevent inadvertent errors in your processing.

Next, we explore the use of local variables and locally dimensioned arrays.

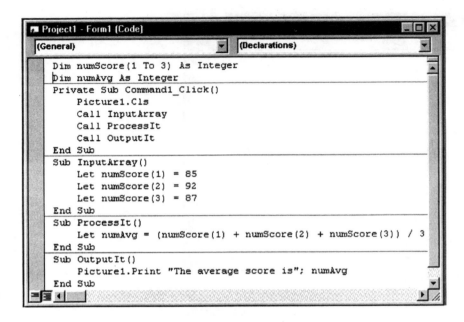

```
Project1 - Form1 [Code]                                    _ □ ×
(General)                    ▼   (Declarations)                ▼
    Dim numScore(1 To 3) As Integer                            ▲
    Dim numAvg As Integer
    Private Sub Command1_Click()
        Picture1.Cls
        Call InputArray
        Call ProcessIt
        Call OutputIt
    End Sub
    Sub InputArray()
        Let numScore(1) = 85
        Let numScore(2) = 92
        Let numScore(3) = 87
    End Sub
    Sub ProcessIt()
        Let numAvg = (numScore(1) + numScore(2) + numScore(3)) / 3
    End Sub
    Sub OutputIt()
        Picture1.Print "The average score is"; numAvg
    End Sub                                                     ▼
```

Figure 9-6. A global variable and a global array used with subroutines.

Exercise 9-3

1. Using subroutines, create the following programs (refer to the programs you did for Exercise 8–2): Given the following flight schedule,

Flight	Origin	Destination	Departure Time
117	Tucson	Dallas	8:45 a.m.
239	LA	Boston	10:15 a.m.
298	Albany	Reno	1:35 p.m.
326	Houston	New York	2:40 p.m.
445	New York	Tampa	4:20 p.m.

write a program to load this information into four arrays of range 1 to 5, *flightNum( )*, *orig( )*, *dest( )*, and *deptTime( )*, and ask the user to request a flight number. Have the computer find the flight number, and display the information corresponding to that flight. Account for the case where the user requests a nonexistent flight.

2. Dimension the string array *stooges( )* with subscripts ranging from 1 to 3 so that the array is visible only to the event procedure cmdStooges_Click. Assign the three values Moe, Larry, Curly to the array as soon as the command button is clicked.

9-4. Passing Variables (Local Variables) and Arrays

Local variables are variables that are used within the main or a subroutine, are variables declared at some location other than the *General Declarations* section, and are variables whose value can be altered and used only within that procedure, unless the value is properly passed to another subroutine.

Passing is a task performed when the value for a variable is transmitted between subroutines, between the main and a subroutine, or between the subroutine and the main. Passing is essential to the creation and proper use of *local variables*.

The general form for passing variables is:

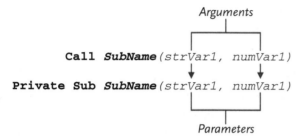

Arguments are the variables or constants appearing in the parenthesis of a *Call* statement. It does not matter whether that *Call* is in the main or a subroutine, the constants or variables within the parenthesis are arguments.

Parameters are variables that appear in the parenthesis in the heading of a subroutine. They accept values from a *Call* statement and transmit back values for each parameter.

It is entirely possible that a value of zero or null is being passed between the procedures. The challenge is to make sure that you are aware of what the value if the variable is when passed to the subroutine, and what it is when passed back to the calling routine. Consider the following:

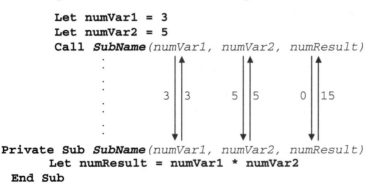

In the above example, the value of *numVar1* and *numVar2* going into the subroutine are 3 and 5 respectively. Note that the subroutine does not change the values, just use them in a calculation. The value for *numResult* is zero going into the subroutine because its value has not been determined. After the subroutine is executed, *numResult* is 15, which is passed back to the main. Note that in order to pass the value for *numResult* back to the main, it had to be in the calling statement even though it had not been used up to that point.

To truly utilize the power of local variables, you would use different names for the variables, both in the arguments and in the parameters. For instance, consider the following program segment:

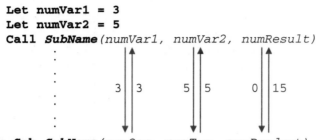

```
Let numVar1 = 3
Let numVar2 = 5
Call SubName(numVar1, numVar2, numResult)
        .
        .             3  3    5  5    0  15
        .
        .
        .
Private Sub SubName(numOne, numTwo, numProduct)
       Let numProduct = numOne * numTwo
   End Sub
```

As you can see from this example, the same values are being used, but they are being passed between two sets of variables with different names. The result of the two programs would be exactly the same, but note that *numProduct*, *numOne*, and *numTwo* are local only to the *SubName* subroutine. If they are used anywhere else in the program, their value does not necessarily have to be the same as the values used in *SubName*.

This is a perfect time to impart the three **Golden Rules of Passing Variables.**

1. *You must pass the same number of variables.* If three variables are being passed from the main, the subprocedure must also have three variables available to accept them, and to transmit values back.

2. *You must pass the same type of variables.* Transmission of a string variable must be met with a string variable in the subroutine, and a numeric met with a numeric. To mix the types is possible on a rare occasion, but it always dangerous.

3. *You must have the variables in the same order.* If the three variables being passed from the main are string, numeric, and string, then the subroutine must also have the variables in that exact same order—string, numeric, and string. This is not usually a problem when dealing with only one variable.

Figure 9-7 uses the same program used for global variables in Figure 9-5, but it does not use the *General Declarations* section to declare variables. Instead, all variables are passed from routine to routine. Note that not all variables are required for all routines.

The outcome of the program in Figure 9-7 would remain the same using the same input, even when the variable names are changed within the subroutines. To illustrate this, consider Figure 9-8.

None of the variables in any of the subroutines are the same in Figure 9-8, yet the program executes as well as the one in Figure 9-7. The keys to success in passing variables are to first pay close attention to the *three Golden Rules of Passing Variables*, and secondly to be sure you are using the same variables in the subroutine as those listed in the parameters for that subroutine.

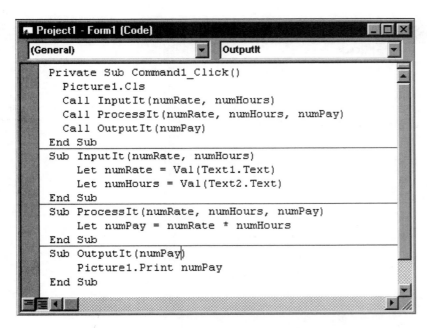

Figure 9-7. Passing variables among routines using the same variable names.

Finally, it is possible to use expressions, constants, and other programming "tricks" when passing variables or assigning values to variables. If you can use local variables properly and not get lost or confused in the process, you will have done well indeed, and you will not need any of the tricks.

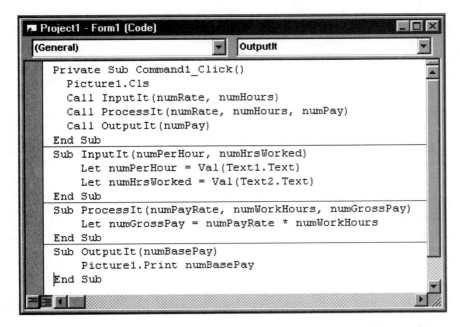

Figure 9-8. Passing variables among subroutines using variables with different names.

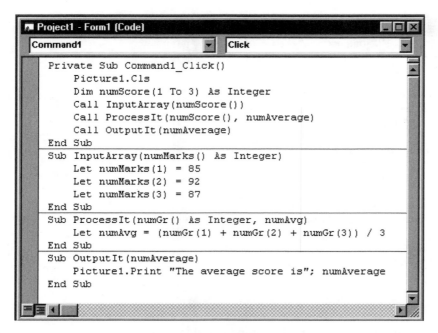

Figure 9-9. Passing arrays between procedures.

Passing Arrays

An array that is not dimensioned in the General Declarations section but is declared in a procedure is local to that procedure and unknown in all other procedures. However, an entire local array can be passed to another procedure. The name of the array, *followed by an empty set of parenthesis*, must appear as an argument in the calling statement. An array variable name of the same type must appear as a corresponding parameter in the subroutine's "Private Sub" statement of the procedure that is to receive the array. In fact, not only is the logic exactly the same as that used for passing variables, the Golden Rules of Passing Variables apply to passing arrays as well. An example of passing arrays is shown in Figure 9-9.

Note that the array variable has an empty subscript. That way, the entire array is passed instead of just one element. You could pass one element by stating which subscripted variable is to be used, but the program would lose its flexibility.

Note also that the array is dimensioned in the procedure in which it will reside.

Exercise 9-4

Revise the two programs you did for Section 9-3, questions 1 and 2. Remove the Dim statements from the General Comments section and make all arrays local arrays. To use them in your subroutines, you will have to pass them in their entirety.

APPENDIX A

USER INTERFACE SKILLS

A-1. USING WINDOWS

Programs such as Visual Basic, which are designed for Microsoft Windows, are supposed to be easy to use—and they are, once you learn a little jargon and a few basic techniques. This section explains the jargon, giving you enough of an understanding of Windows to get you started in Visual Basic. Although Windows may seem intimidating if you've never used it before, you need to learn only a few basic techniques, which are covered right here.

Mouse Pointers

When you use Windows, think of yourself as the conductor and Windows as the orchestra. The conductor in an orchestra points to various members, does something with his or her baton, and then the orchestra members respond in certain ways. For a Windows user, the baton is called the **pointing device**; most often it is a **mouse**. The idea is that as you move the mouse across your desk, a pointer moves along the screen in sync with your movements. Two basic types of mouse pointers you will see in Windows are an arrow and an hourglass.

The **arrow** is the ordinary mouse pointer you use to point at various Windows objects before activating them. You will usually be instructed to "Move the pointer to . . ." This really means "Move the mouse around your desk until the mouse pointer is at . . .

The **hourglass** mouse pointer pops up whenever Windows is saying: "Wait a minute; I'm thinking." This pointer still moves around when you move the mouse, but you can't tell Windows to do anything until it finishes what it's doing and the mouse pointer no longer resembles an hourglass. (Sometimes you can press the Esc key to tell Windows to stop what it is doing.)

NOTE: The mouse pointer can take on many other shapes, depending on which document you are using and what task you are performing. For instance, when entering text in a word processor or Visual Basic, the mouse pointer appears as a thin, large, uppercase I (referred to as an I-Beam).

Mouse Actions

After you move the (arrow) pointer to a place where you want something to happen, you need to do something with the mouse. There are four basic things you can do with a mouse—point, click, double-click, and drag.

Pointing means moving your mouse across your desk until the mouse pointer is over the desired object on the screen.

Clicking (sometimes people say single-clicking) means pressing and releasing the left mouse button once. Whenever a sentence begins "Click on . . . ," you need to

1. Move the mouse pointer until it is at the object you are supposed to click on.

2. Press and release the left mouse button.

An example of a sentence using this jargon might be "Click on the button marked Yes." You also will see sentences that begin "Click inside the . . . This means to move the mouse pointer until it is inside the boundaries of the object, and then click.

Double-clicking means clicking the left mouse button twice in quick succession (that is, pressing it, releasing it, pressing it, and releasing it again quickly so that Windows doesn't think you single-clicked twice). Whenever a sentence begins "Double-click on . . . ," you need to

1. Move the mouse pointer until it is at the object you are supposed to double-click on.

2. Press and release the left mouse button twice in quick succession.

For example, you might be instructed to "Double-click on the little box at the far left side of your screen."

NOTE: An important Windows convention is that clicking selects an object so you can give Windows or the document further directions about it, but double-clicking tells Windows (or the document) to do something.

Dragging usually moves a Windows object. If you see a sentence that begins "Drag the . . . ," you need to

1. Move the mouse pointer until it is at the object.
2. Press the left mouse button, and hold it down.
3. Now move the mouse pointer until the object moves to where you want it to be.
4. Finally, release the mouse button.

Sometimes this whole activity is called *drag and drop*.

Starting Windows

Windows starts automatically when you turn on your computer After a little delay, you will first see the Windows logo and finally a screen looking something like Figure A-1 . The little pictures (with labels) are called **icons**. You double-click on the My Computer icon to see your computer's contents and manage your files. You click on the **Start button** (at the bottom left corner of the screen) to run programs such as Visual Basic, end Windows, and carry out several other tasks. (The Start menu also can be accessed with Ctrl+Esc.)

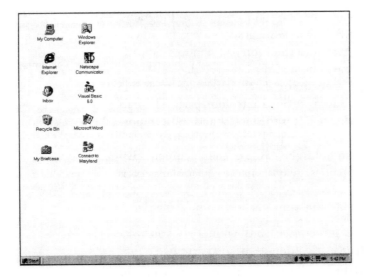

Figure A-1 Windows desktop

Windows and Its Little Windows

Windows gets its name from the way it organizes your screen into rectangular regions. When you run a program, the program runs inside a bordered rectangular box. Unfortunately Windows jargon calls all of these windows, so there's only a lowercase "w" to distinguish them from the program called Windows.

When Windows' attentions are focused on a specific window, the bar at the top of the window is highlighted and the window is said to be **active**. The active window is the only one that can be affected by your actions. An example of a sentence you might see is "Make the window active." This means that if the title bar of the window is not already highlighted, click inside the window. At this point, the (new) window will be responsive to your actions.

Using the Notepad

We will explore the Windows application Notepad to illustrate the Windows environment. The Notepad is used extensively in this text to create data files for programs. Most of the concepts learned here carry over to Visual Basic and other Windows applications.

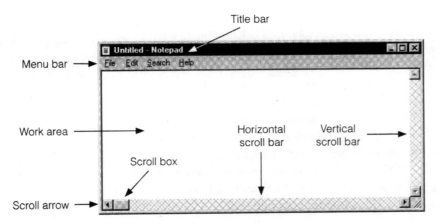

Figure A-2 The Notepad window.

To invoke Notepad from Windows click the Start button, point to Programs, point to Accessories and click Notepad. As its name suggests, Notepad is an elementary word processor. You can type text into the Notepad window, edit the text, print the text on the printer, and save the text for later recall.

The blinking vertical line is called the **cursor**. Each letter you type will appear at the cursor. The Notepad window is divided into four parts. The part containing the cursor is called the **Work area**. It is the largest and most important part of the window because documents are typed into this window.

The **Title bar** at the top of the screen holds the name of the document currently being written. Until the document is given a name, the document is called "Untitled."

You can change the window to exactly suit your needs. To adjust the size

1. Move the mouse pointer until it is at the place on the boundary you want to adjust. The mouse pointer changes to a double-headed arrow.

2. Drag the border to the left or right or up or down to make it smaller or larger.

3. When you are satisfied with the new size of the window, release the left mouse button.

If the Work area contains more information than can fit on the screen, you need a way to move through this information so you can see it all. For example, you will certainly be writing instructions in Visual Basic that are longer than one screen. You can use the mouse to march through your instructions with small steps or giant steps. A **Vertical scroll bar** lets you move from the top to the bottom of the window; a **Horizontal scroll bar** lets you move within the left and right margins of the window. Use this Scroll bar when the contents of the window are too wide to fit on the screen. Figure A-2 shows both Vertical and Horizontal scroll bars.

A scroll bar has two arrows at the end of a channel and sometimes contains a box (usually called the **Scroll box**). The Scroll box is the key to moving rapidly; the arrows are the key to moving in smaller increments. Dragging the Scroll box enables you to quickly move long distances to an approximate location in your document. For example, if you drag the Scroll box to the middle of the channel, you'll scroll to approximately the middle of your document.

The **Menu bar** just below the Title bar is used to call up menus, or lists of tasks. Several of these tasks are described in this section.

Documents are created from the keyboard in much the same way they would be written with a typewriter. In computerese, writing a document is referred to as editing the document; therefore, the Notepad is called a **text editor**. Before discussing editing, we must first examine the workings of the keyboard.

There are several different styles of keyboards. Figure A-3 shows a typical one. The keyboard is divided into several parts. The largest portion looks and functions like an ordinary typewriter keyboard. Above this portion are twelve keys labeled Fl through F12, called the **function keys**. (On many keyboards, the function keys are located on the left side.) Function keys are used to perform certain tasks with a single keystroke. For instance, pressing the function key F5 displays the time and date. The right portion of the keyboard, called the **numeric keypad**, is used either to move the cursor or to enter numbers. Press the **Num Lock** key a few times and notice the tiny light labeled NUM LOCK blink on and off. When the light is on, the numeric keypad produces numbers;

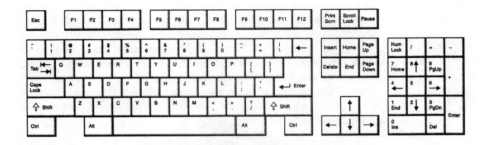

Figure A-3. IBM PC keyboard.

otherwise, it moves the cursor. The Num Lock key is called a toggle key because it "toggles" between two states. When the numeric keypad is in the cursor-moving state, the four arrow keys each move the cursor around the existing document.

Two very important keys may not have names printed on them. The **Enter** key is the key with the hooked arrow (and/or the word Enter). It corresponds to the carriage return on a typewriter, and is used to start a new line of a document. The **Backspace** key is the gray key with the left-pointing arrow located above the Enter key. It moves the cursor one space to the left and erases any character in that location.

After the Notepad has been invoked, the following routine will introduce you to the keyboard.

1. Click on the Work area of the Notepad.

2. Type a few words into the Notepad.

3. Use the right and left cursor-moving keys on the numeric keypad to move the cursor.

4. Press the **Home** key to move the cursor back to the beginning of the line. In general, the Home key moves the cursor to the beginning of the line on which it currently is located.

5. Now press the **End** key (on the numeric keypad). The cursor will move to the end of the line.

6. Type some letters using the central typewriter portion of the keyboard. The two **Shift** keys are used to obtain uppercase letters or the upper character of keys showing two characters.

7. Press the **Caps Lock** key and then type some letters. The letters will appear in uppercase. We say the keyboard is in uppercase mode. To toggle back to lowercase mode, press the Caps Lock key again. Only alphabetic keys are affected by Caps Lock.

NOTE: When the keyboard is in the uppercase state, the tiny light labeled CAPS LOCK on the keyboard is lit.

8. Type some letters and then press the Backspace key a few times. It will erase letters one at a time. Another method of deleting a letter is to move the cursor to that letter and press the **Del** key. (Del stands for "Delete.")

The backspace key erases the character to the left of the cursor, and the Del key erases the character to the right of the cursor

9. Hold down the **Ctrl** key (Ctrl stands for "Control"), and press the **Del** key. This combination erases the portion of the line to the right of the cursor. We describe this combination as **Ctrl + Del**. (The plus sign indicates that the Ctrl key is to be held down while pressing the Del key.) There are many useful key combinations like this.

10. Type a few letters and use the appropriate cursor-moving key to move the cursor in front of one of the letters. Now type any letter. Notice that it is inserted at the cursor position and that the letters following it move to the right. This is because the Notepad uses **insert mode**. Visual Basic has an additional mode, called **overwrite mode**, in which a typed letter overwrites the letter located at the cursor position. In Visual Basic, overwrite mode is invoked by pressing the **Ins** key. (Ins stands for "Insert.") Pressing this toggle key again reinstates insert mode. The cursor size indicates the active mode; a large cursor means overwrite mode.

11. The key to the left of the Q key is called the **Tab** key. It is marked with a pair of arrows, the upper one pointing to the left and the lower one pointing to the right. At the beginning of the line, pressing the Tab key indents the cursor several spaces.

12. Type more characters than can fit on one line of the screen. Notice that the leftmost characters scroll off the screen to make room for the new characters.

13. The Enter key is used to begin a new line on the screen in much the same way that the carriage return lever is used on a manual typewriter.

14. The **Alt** key activates the Menu bar. Then, pressing one of the underlined letters, such as F, E, S, or H, selects a menu. (From the Menu bar, a menu can also be selected by pressing the right-arrow key to highlight the name and then pressing the Enter key.) As shown in Figure A-4, after a menu is opened, each option has one letter underlined. You can press an underlined letter to select an option. (Underlined letters are called **access keys**.) For instance, pressing A from the file menu selects the option "Save As". Selections also can be made with the cursor-moving keys and the Enter key.

NOTE 1: You can select menus and options without the use of keys by clicking on them with the mouse.

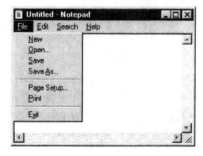

Figure A-4. A menu and its options.

NOTE 2: You can close a menu, without making a selection by clicking anywhere outside the menu or pressing the Esc key twice.

---

15. The **Esc** key (Esc stands for "Escape") is used to return to the Work area.

16. Press and release Alt, then press and release F and then press N. (This key combination is abbreviated Alt/File/New or Alt/F/N.) The dialog box in Figure A-5 will appear and ask you if you want to save the current document. Decline by pressing N or clicking on the No button.

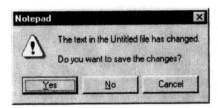

Figure A-5. A "Do you want to save the changes?" dialog box.

17. Type the following information into the Notepad. (It gives the names of employees, their hourly wages, and the number of hours worked in the past week.) This document is used in Section 3-5. ~~3-5.~~

NOTE: We follow the convention of surrounding words with quotation marks to distinguish words from numbers, which are written without quotation marks.

"MikeJones", 7.35,35
"John Smith", 6.75, 33

18. Let's store the document as a file on a disk. To save the document, press Alt/File/Save As. A dialog box appears to request a file name for the document (see Figure A-6). The cursor is in a narrow rectangular box labeled "File name:".

Type a drive letter, a colon, and a name, and then press the Enter key or click on Save. For instance, you might type A:STAFF. The document will then be stored on drive A. This process is called **saving** the document. Notepad automatically adds a period and the extension txt to the name. Therefore, the complete file name is STAFF.TXT on the disk.

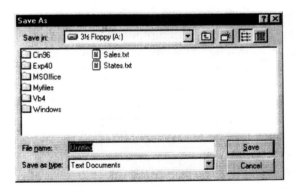

Figure A-6. Save As dialog box.

NOTE: If you want to save the document in a specific folder (directory) of the disk, also type the folder (directory). For instance, you might type A: \ MYFILES \ STAFF

NOTE: You can move around in any dialog box by repeatedly pressing the Tab key.)

19. Press the key combination Alt/File/New to clear STAFFTXT from Notepad.

20. Restore STAFF.TXT as the document in the Notepad by pressing Alt/File/Open, typing STAFF (possibly preceded by a drive letter and a colon, such as A:, and a folder) at the cursor position, and then pressing the Enter key.

21. Move the cursor to the beginning of the document, and then press Alt/S/F to invoke the Find dialog box. This dialog box contains several objects that will be discussed in this book. The text to be found should be typed into the rectangle containing the cursor. Such a rectangle is called a text box. The phrase "Find what:", which identifies the type of information that should be placed into the text box, is referred to as the caption of a label.

22. Type "smith" into the text box and then click on the "Find Next" button. This button is an example of a command button. Clicking on it carries out a task.

23. The small square to the left of the words "Match case" is called a check box. Click on it to see it checked, and then click again to remove the check mark.

24. The object captioned "Direction" is called a frame. It contains a pair of objects called option buttons. Click on the "Up" option button to select it, and then click on the "Down" option button. Only one option button at a time can be selected.

25. Press Alt/File/Exit to exit Notepad.

Ending Windows

To close Windows, click the Start button and then click Shut Down. You are presented with a message box that looks like the window in FigureA.7 Click Yes. (If you forgot to save changes to documents, Windows will prompt you to save changes.) A screen message might appear to let you know when you can safely turn off your computer.

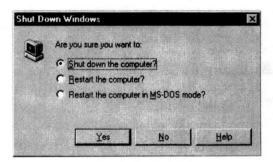

Figure A-7. Dialog box for ending Windows.

Comments

1. The key sequences discussed in this section follow the format keyl+key2 or keyl/key2. The plus sign (+) instructs you to hold down key1 and then press key2. The slash symbol (/) tells you to release key1 before pressing key2. Some useful key combinations that we have not discussed yet are the following:

    (a) Ctrl+Home: moves the cursor to the beginning of the document

    (b) Ctrl+End: moves the cursor to the end of the document

    (c) Alt/F/P/Enter: prints a copy of the current document on the printer

2. When the work area is completely filled with lines of text, the document scrolls upward to accommodate additional lines. The lines that have scrolled off the top can be viewed again by pressing the **PgUp** key. The **PgDn** key moves farther down the document.

3. There are several ways to clear the work area. You can either erase the lines one at a time with Ctrl+Del, select the entire document with Alt/E/A and then erase all lines simultaneously with Del, or begin a new document with Alt/F/N. With the last method, a dialog box may query you about saving the current document. In this case, use Tab to select the desired option and press the Enter key. The document name in the Title bar will change to Untitled.

4. Notepad can perform many of the tasks of word processors such as search and block operations. However, these features needn't concern us presently.

5. TXT is the default extension for files created with Notepad.

6. The title bar of the Notepad window, or of any window, contains buttons that can be used to maximize, minimize, or close the window. See Figure A-8.

    You can click on the Maximize button to make the Notepad window fill the entire screen, click on the Minimize button to change the Notepad window into a button on the taskbar, or click on the Close button to exit Notepad. As long as a window isn't maximized or minimized, you can usually move it around the screen by dragging its title bar. (Recall that this means to move the mouse pointer until it is in the title bar, hold down the left mouse button, move the mouse until the window is where you want it to be, and then release the mouse button.)

Figure A-8. Title bar of the Notepad window.

NOTE 1: If you have maximized a window, the Maximize button changes to a pair of rectangles called the **Restore button**. Click on this button to return the window to its previous size.

NOTE 2: If the Notepad window has been minimized, it can be restored to its previous size by clicking on the button that was created on the task bar when the Minimize button was clicked.

7. You should end Windows by the procedures discussed in this section whenever possible. It is a bad idea to end Windows by just shutting off your machine.

A-2. DISKS AND FOLDERS

Modern computers have a hard disk, a diskette drive, and usually a CD drive. The hard disk is permanently housed inside the computer. You can read information from all three drives, but can only write information to the hard disk and to diskettes. Most diskette drives accommodate the type of diskette shown in Figure A-9. This diskette has a plastic jacket and measures 3½" in width.

When the diskette is inserted into a drive, the shutter slides to the right and exposes the read-write window. The diskette drive records and reads data through the read-write window. The write-protect hole is normally covered. When the write-protect hole is uncovered by sliding the slider on the back of the diskette, nothing can be erased from or recorded on the diskette. To insert a diskette, hold the diskette with the label facing up and the read/write window pointing toward the diskette drive. You insert the diskette by just pushing

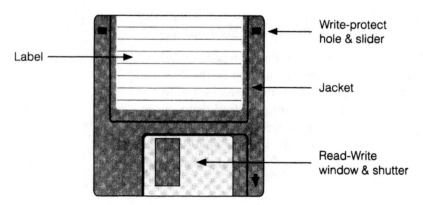

Figure A-9. 3 1/2" diskette.

it into the drive until you hear a click. You remove it by pressing the button on the drive.

When handling a diskette, be careful not to touch the exposed surface in the read-write window. Also, do not remove a diskette from a diskette drive while the little light on the diskette drive is lit.

We use the word **disk** to refer to either the hard disk, a diskette, or a CD. Each drive is identified by a letter. Normally the hard drive is identified by C, the diskette by A, and the CD drive by D or E.

Disk management is handled by the computer's operating system. VB 6.0 requires that your computer use a Windows 95, Windows 98, or Windows NT 4.0 (or later) operating system.

Disks hold not only programs but also corrections of data stored in **data files**. The term file refers to either a data file or a program file. Each file has a name consisting of a base name followed by an optional extension consisting of a period and one or more characters. Letters, digits, spaces, periods, and a few other assorted characters (see Comment 1) can be used in file names. Extensions are normally used to identify the type of file. For example, spreadsheets created with Excel have the extension xls, documents created with Word have the extension doc, and files created with Notepad have the extension txt. Some examples of file names are "Annual Sales.xls," 'Letter to Mom.doc, and "Phone.txt".

Because a disk is capable of holding thousands of files, locating a specific file can be quite time-consuming. Therefore, related files are grouped into collections that are stored in separate areas of the disk. For instance, one area might hold all your Visual Basic programs, and another the documents created with your word processor.

Think of a disk as a large folder, called the **root folder**, that contains several smaller folders, each with its own name. (The naming of folders follows the same rule as the naming of files.) Each of these smaller folders can contain yet other named folders. Each folder is identified by listing its name preceded by the names of the successively larger folders that contain it, with each folder name preceded by a backslash. Such a sequence is called a **path**. For instance, the path \SALES\NY.98\JULY identifies the folder JULY, contained in the folder NY.98, which in turn is contained in the folder SALES. Think of a file, along with its name, as written on a slip of paper that can be placed into either the root folder or one of the smaller folders. The combination of a drive letter followed by a colon, a path, and a file name is called a **filespec**, an abbreviation of "file specification." Some examples of filespecs are C:\VB9S\VB.EXE and A: \ PERSONAL \ INCOME99.TXT.

In DOS and earlier versions of Windows, folders were called directories. Many Visual Basic objects and commands still refer to folders as directories. Windows contains two programs (My Computer and Windows Explorer) that help you view, organize, and manage the folders and files on your disks. We will carry out these tasks with My Computer We will learn how to create, rename, copy, move, and delete folders and files.

Using My Computer

To invoke My Computer, double-click on the My Computer icon. Your initial window will show an icon for each drive (and a few other icons). If you double-click on one of the drive icons a second window containing the folders and

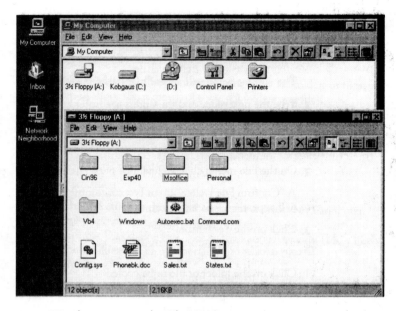

Figure A-10. Windows created with My Computer.

files for that drive will appear. Figure A-10 shows a possible pair of windows. A folder is identified by a folder icon, a file created with Notepad is identified by a small spiral notepad, and an executable file is identified by a rectangle (with a thin bar across top) icon.

To open a folder, double click on that folder. A window with the folder's name in its title bar will appear. This window will contain an icon for each subfolder and file of the original folder. Figure A-11 shows such a window.

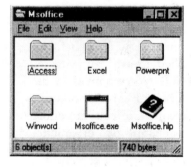

Figure A-11. A window produced by opening a folder.

To create a new folder:

1. Open the folder that is to contain the new folder as a subfolder

---

NOTE: Initially, the root folder is open.

---

2. On the File menu, point to New, and then click Folder (Or press Alt/File/New/Folder.)

    The new folder appears with a temporary name.

3. Type a name for the folder and then press the Enter key.

To rename a folder or file:

1. Click on the folder or file.

2. On the File menu, click Rename. (Or press Alt/File/Rename.) The current name will appear highlighted inside a rectangle.

3. Type the new name and then press the Enter key.

To delete a folder or file:

1. Click on the folder or file.

2. On the File menu, click Delete. (Or press Alt/File/Delete or Del.)

    A "Confirm File Delete" input box containing the name of the folder or file will appear.

3. Click on the Yes button.

To copy a folder or file:

1. Click on the folder or file to be copied.

2. On the Edit menu, click Copy. (Or press Alt/Edit/Copy.)

3. Open the folder or disk where the copy is to be placed.

4. On the Edit menu, click Paste. (Or press Alt/Edit/Paste.)

To move a folder or file:

1. Click on the folder or file to be moved.

2. On the Edit menu, click on Cut. (Or press Alt/Edit/Cut.)

3. Open the folder where the folder or file is to be placed.

4. On the Edit menu, click Paste. (Or press Alt/Edit/Paste.)

    You also can carry out some of the preceding operations by "drag and drop." For details, see the Help Topics accessed through the My Computer Help menu. For instance, you can delete a folder or file by dragging it to the Recycle Bin and releasing the left mouse button.

Comments

1. File names can consist of digits, letters of the alphabet, spaces, and the characters & ! _ @ ' ' ~ ( ) { } −# % . + , ; = [ ] $.

2. File names can consist of up to 255 characters including spaces. However, a name cannot contain the following characters: \ /: ? ★ " > < |

3. Names of folders do not usually have an extension.

4. Neither Windows nor Visual Basic distinguishes between uppercase and lower-case letters in folders and file names. For instance, the names

COSTS99.TXT, Costs99.Txt, and costs99.txt are equivalent. From now on, we will use uppercase letters in this book.

5. Because you cannot write to a CD drive, you cannot rename or delete files or folders residing on a CD drive.

6. When you delete a folder directory containing other subfolders or files, you will be queried about the removal of these subfolders and files.

7. Most diskettes purchased these days are "preformatted." Formatting prepares the disk for use with your computer and deletes any previous information stored on it. If you have a diskette that has not been formatted, you must format it yourself before you can use it.

To format a diskette:

    (a) Insert the diskette in a drive, and select the drive in My Computer

    (b) From the File menu, choose Format.

    (c) In the Format Disk dialog box, specify the various options. (Most likely, the default values will be appropriate.)

    (d) Click the Start button.

8. You can obtain further information about My Computer by selecting "Search for Help on" from its Help menu and then specifying a topic.

9. Suppose you typed A:\MYFILES\STAFF into the "File_name:" box. The disk drive and directory could have been specified with other parts of the dialog box.

    (a) Click on the arrow to the right of the "Save_in:" box and click on "3 1/2 Floppy (A:)" to select the A: drive.

The large box in the center of the "Save As" window shows the subfolder of the selected drive.

    (b) Open the desired folder by double-clicking on it.

The folder will replace the drive in the "Save in:" box and its subfolders will appear in the large box. This process can be repeated as many times as required to locate the desired folder

    (c) Return to the "File name:" box and type in STAFF.

    (d) Press the Enter key or click on the Save button.

10. There are many uses of dialog boxes such as the one discussed in comment 9. For instance, they pop up to report errors in a Visual Basic document. In general, the Tab key is used to move around inside a dialog box and the Enter key makes a selection. Although dialog boxes often have a cancel button, the Esc key also can be used to remove the dialog box from the screen.

11. In DOS and early versions of Windows, file names were limited to no more than eight characters followed by an optional extension of at most 3 characters. This is referred to as the 8.3 format. In this text we use the 8.3 format so that folders also can be explored in DOS, and with all utility programs.

12. Some books use the word "path" to mean what we call "filespec."

A-3.   Installing the Working Model Edition of Visual Basic

1. Place the CD accompanying this book into your CD drive.

2. Wait about five seconds. You will most likely hear a whirring sound from the CD drive and then a large window with the words "Visual Basic 6.0 Working Model" will appear. If so, go to Step 5.

3. If nothing happens automatically after Step 1, double-click on My Computer in the Windows Desktop.

4. A window showing the different disk drives will appear. Double-click on the icon containing a picture of a CD (along with a drive) and having the drive letter below the label. A large window with the words "Visual Basic 6.0 Working Model" will appear.

5. The title bar of the large window says "Installation Wizard for Visual Basic 6.0 Working Model." The installation wizard will guide you through the installation process. Click on Next to continue.

6. An End User License Agreement will appear. After reading the agreement, click on the the circle to the left of the sentence "I accept the agreement." and then click on Next.

7. The next window to appear has spaces for an ID number, your name, and your company's name. Ignore the ID number. Just type in your name and, optionally, a company name, and then click Next.

8. Visual Basic 6.0 requires that you have Internet Explorer 4.0 or later version on your computer. If a recent version is not present, the Installation Wizard will install it for you. If so, successive windows will guide you through the installation. At some point you will be required to restart your computer. We recommend doing the standard installation and using the recommended destination folder.

9. You will next be guided through the installation of DCOM9S, which is also needed to Visual Basic 6.0. After installing DCOM9S, the installation wizard will automatically restart your computer and then continue with the installation of VB6.0. Note: If another widow is covering the Installation Wizard window, then click on the Installation Wizard window. If you can't find the Installation Wizard window, repeat Steps 1-5.

   You will now be guided through the installation of the Working Model Edition VB6.0. At the end of the installation, Visual Basic will be invoked.

10. The next window requests the name of the Common Install Folder. We recommend that you simply click on Next, which will accept the default folder and copy some files into it.

11. The next window to appear is the Visual Basic 6.0 Working Model Setup. Click on Continue.

12. The next screen shows your Product ID number. Enter your name and then click on OK.

13. The next window asks you to choose between Typical and Custom installations. We recommend that you click on the Typical icon.

14. About one minute is required for the VB6.0 Working Model to be installed. On the next screen to appear, click on Restart Windows.

15. The next window to appear gives you the opportunity to register your copy of VB6.0 over the web. Uncheck the Register Now box and click on Finish.

Invoke Visual Basic after installation.

16. Click the Start button.
17. Point to Programs.
18. Point to Microsoft Visual Basic 6.0. (A new panel will open on the right.)
19. In the new panel, click on Microsoft Visual Basic 6.0.

Exit Visual Basic.

20. Press the Esc key.
21. Press Alt/F/X.
22. If an unsaved program is present, Visual Basic will prompt you about saving it.

NOTE: In many situations, Step 20 is not needed.

Accompanying CD

The CD in this book contains the files needed to install the Working Model Edition of Visual Basic 6.0. To install the software, follow the steps in Appendix A-3.

End-User License Agreement for Microsoft Software

IMPORTANT—READ CAREFULLY: This Microsoft End-User License Agreement ("EULA") is a legal agreement between you (either an individual or a single entity) and Microsoft Corporation for the Microsoft software product identified above, which includes computer software and may include associated media, printed materials, and "online" or electronic documentation ("SOFTWARE PRODUCT"). The SOFTWARE PRODUCT also includes any updates and supplements to the original SOFTWARE PRODUCT provided to you by Microsoft. Any software provided along with the SOFTWARE PRODUCT that is associated with a separate end-user license agreement is licensed to you under the terms of that license agreement. By installing, copying, downloading, accessing or otherwise using the SOFTWARE PRODUCT, you agree to be bound by the terms of this EULA. If you do not agree to the terms of this EULA, do not install, copy, or otherwise use the SOFTWARE PRODUCT.

Software Product License

The SOFTWARE PRODUCT is protected by copyright laws and international copyright treaties, as well as other intellectual property laws and treaties. The SOFTWARE PRODUCT is licensed, not sold.

1. **GRANT OF LICENSE.** This EULA grants you the following rights:

   1.1 **License Grant.** You may install and use one copy of the SOFTWARE PRODUCT on a single computer. You may also store or install a copy of the SOFTWARE PRODUCT on a storage device, such as a network server, used only to install or run the SOFTWARE PRODUCT over an internal network; however, you must acquire and dedicate a license for each separate computer on or from which the SOFTWARE PRODUCT is installed, used, accessed, displayed or run.

   1.2 **Academic Use.** You must be a "Qualified Educational User" to use the SOFTWARE PRODUCT in the manner described in this section. To determine whether you are a Qualified Educational User, please contact the Microsoft Sales Information Center/One Microsoft Way/Redmond, WA 98052-6399 or the Microsoft subsidiary serving your country. If you are a Qualified Educational User, you may either:

      (i) exercise the rights granted in Section 1.1, OR

      (ii) if you intend to use the SOFTWARE PRODUCT solely for instructional purposes in connection with a class or other educational program, this EULA grants you the following alternative license models:

      (A) Per Computer Model. For every valid license you have acquired for the SOFTWARE PRODUCT, you may install a single copy of the SOFTWARE PRODUCT on a single computer for access and use by an unlimited number of student end users at your educational institution, provided that all such end users comply with all other terms of this EULA, OR

      (B) Per License Model. If you have multiple licenses for the SOFTWARE PRODUCT, then at any time you may have as many copies of the SOFTWARE PRODUCT in use as you have licenses, provided that such use is limited to student or faculty end users at your educational institution and provided that all such end users comply with all other terms of this EULA. For purposes of this subsection, the SOFTWARE PRODUCT is "in use" on a computer when it is loaded into the temporary memory (i.e., RAM) or installed into the permanent memory (e.g., hard disk, CD ROM, or other storage device) of that computer, except that a copy installed on a network server for the sole purpose of distribution to other computers is not 'in use'. If the anticipated number of users of the

SOFTWARE PRODUCT will exceed the number of applicable licenses, then you must have a reasonable mechanism or process in place to ensure that the number of persons using the SOFTWARE PRODUCT concurrently does not exceed the number of licenses.

2. DESCRIPTION OF OTHER RIGHTS AND LIMITATIONS.

- **Limitations on Reverse Engineering, Decompilation, and Disassembly.** You may not reverse engineer, decompile, or disassemble the SOFTWARE PRODUCT, except and only to the extent that such activity is expressly permitted by applicable law notwithstanding this limitation.

- **Separation of Components.** The SOFTWARE PRODUCT is licensed as a single product. Its component parts may not be separated for use on more than one computer.

- **Rental.** You may not rent, lease or lend the SOFTWARE PRODUCT.

- **Trademarks.** This EULA does not grant you any rights in connection with any trademarks or service marks of Microsoft

- **Software Transfer.** The initial user of the SOFTWARE PRODUCT may make a one-time permanent transfer of this EULA and SOFTWARE PRODUCT only directly to an end user. This transfer must include all of the SOFTWARE PRODUCT (including all component parts, the media and printed materials, any upgrades, this EULA, and, if applicable, the Certificate of Authenticity). Such transfer may not be by way of consignment or any other indirect transfer The transferee of such one-time transfer must agree to comply with the terms of this EULA, including the obligation not to further transfer this EULA and SOFTWARE PRODUCT.

- **Termination.** Without prejudice to any other rights, Microsoft may terminate this EULA if you fail to comply with the terms and conditions of this EULA. In such event, you must destroy all copies of the SOFTWARE PRODUCT and all of its component parts.

4. **COPYRIGHT**. All title and intellectual property rights in and to the SOFTWARE PRODUCT (including but not limited to any images, photographs, animations, video, audio, music, text, and "applets" incorporated into the SOFTWARE PRODUCT), the accompanying printed materials, and any copies of the SOFTWARE PRODUCT are owned by Microsoft or its suppliers. All title and intellectual property rights in and to the content which may be accessed through use of the SOFTWARE PRODUCT is the property of the respective content owner and may be protected by applicable copyright or other intellectual property laws and treaties. This EULA grants you no rights to use such content. All rights not expressly granted are reserved by Microsoft.

5. **BACKUP COPY**. After installation of one copy of the SOFTWARE PRODUCT pursuant to this EULA, you may keep the original media on which the SOFTWARE PRODUCT was provided by Microsoft solely for backup or archival purposes. If the original media is required to use the SOFTWARE PRODUCT on the COMPUTER, you may make one copy of the SOFTWARE PRODUCT solely for backup or archival

purposes. Except as expressly provided in this EULA, you may not otherwise make copies of the SOFTWARE PRODUCT or the printed materials accompanying the SOFTWARE PRODUCT.

6. **U.S. GOVERNMENT RESTRICTED RIGHTS.** The SOFTWARE PRODUCT and documentation are provided with RESTRICTED RIGHTS. Use, duplication, or disclosure by the Government is subject to restrictions as set forth in subparagraph (c)(l)(ii) of the Rights in Technical Data and Computer Software clause at DFARS 252.227-7013 or subparagraphs (c)(1) and (2) of the Commercial Computer Software—Restricted Rights at 48 CFR 52.227-19, as applicable. Manufacturer is Microsoft Corporation/One Microsoft Way/Redmond, WA 98052-6399.

7. **EXPORT RESTRICTIONS.** You agree that you will not export or re-export the SOFTWARE PRODUCT, any part thereof, or any process or service that is the direct product of the SOFTWARE PRODUCT (the foregoing collectively referred to as the "Restricted Components"), to any country, person, entity or end user subject to U.S. export restrictions. You specifically agree not to export or re-export any of the Restricted Components (i) to any country to which the U.S. has embargoed or restricted the export of goods or services, which currently include, but are not necessarily limited to Cuba, Iran, Iraq, Libya, North Korea, Sudan and Syria, or to any national of any such country, wherever located, who intends to transmit or transport the Restricted Components back to such country; (ii) to any end-user who you know or have reason to know will utilize the Restricted Components in the design, development or production of nuclear, chemical or biological weapons; or (iii) to any end-user who has been prohibited from participating in U.S. export transactions by any federal agency of the U.S. government. You warrant and represent that neither the BXA nor any other U.S. federal agency has suspended, revoked, or denied your export privileges.

8. **NOTE ON JAVA SUPPORT.** THE SOFTWARE PRODUCT MAY CONTAIN SUPPORT FOR PROGRAMS WRITTEN IN JAVA. JAVA TECHNOLOGY IS NOT FAULT TOLERANT AND IS NOT DESIGNED, MANUFACTURED, OR INTENDED FOR USE OR RESALE AS ONLINE CONTROL EQUIPMENT IN HAZARDOUS ENVIRONMENTS REQUIRING FAIL-SAFE PERFORMANCE, SUCH AS IN THE OPERATION OF NUCLEAR FACILITIES, AIRCRAFT NAVIGATION OR COMMUNICATION SYSTEMS, AIR TRAFFIC CONTROL, DIRECT LIFE SUPPORT MACHINES, OR WEAPONS SYSTEMS, IN WHICH THE FAILURE OF JAVA TECHNOLOGY COULD LEAD DIRECTLY TO DEATH, PERSONAL INJURY, OR SEVERE PHYSICAL OR ENVIRONMENTAL DAMAGE.

Miscellaneous

If you acquired this product in the United States, this EULA is governed by the laws of the State of Washington.

If you acquired this product in Canada, this EULA is governed by the laws of the Province of Ontario, Canada. Each of the parties hereto irrevocably attorns to the jurisdiction of the courts of the Province of Ontario and further agrees to commence any litigation which may arise hereunder in the courts located in the Judicial District of York, Province of Ontario.

If this product was acquired outside the United States, then local law may apply.

Should you have any questions concerning this EULA, or if you desire to contact Microsoft for any reason, please contact Microsoft, or write: Microsoft Sales Information Center/One Microsoft Way Redmond, WA 98052-6399.

Limited Warranty

LIMITED WARRANTY. Microsoft warrants that (a) the SOFTWARE PRODUCT will perform substantially in accordance with the accompanying written materials for a period of ninety (90) days from the date of receipt, and (b) any Support Services provided by Microsoft shall be substantially as described in applicable written materials provided to you by Microsoft, and Microsoft support engineers will make commercially reasonable efforts to solve any problem. To the extent allowed by applicable law, implied warranties on the SOFTWARE PRODUCT, if any, are limited to ninety (90) days. Some states/jurisdictions do not allow limitations on duration of an implied warranty so the above limitation may not apply to you.

CUSTOMER REMEDIES. Microsoft's and its suppliers' entire liability and your exclusive remedy shall be, at Microsoft's option, either (a) return of the price paid, if any, or (b) repair or replacement of the SOFTWARE PRODUCT that does not meet Microsoft's Limited Warranty and that is returned to Microsoft with a copy of your receipt. This Limited Warranty is void if failure of the SOFTWARE PRODUCT has resulted from accident, abuse, or misapplication. Any replacement SOFTWARE PRODUCT will be warranted for the remainder of the original warranty period or thirty (30) days, whichever is longer. Outside the United States, neither these remedies nor any product support services offered by Microsoft are available without proof of purchase from an authorized international source.

NO OTHER WARRANTIES. To the maximum extent permitted by applicable law, Microsoft and its suppliers disclaim all other warranties and conditions, either express or implied, including, but not limited to, implied warranties OR CONDITIONS of merchantability, fitness for a particular purpose, title and non-infringement, with regard to the SOFTWARE PRODUCT, and the provision of or failure to provide Support Services. This limited warranty gives you specific legal rights. You may have others, which vary from state/jurisdiction to state/jurisdiction.

LIMITATION OF LIABILITY. TO THE MAXIMUM EXTENT PERMITTED BY APPLICABLE LAW, IN NO EVENT SHALL MICROSOFT OR ITS SUPPLIERS BE LIABLE FOR ANY SPECIAL, INCIDENTAL, INDIRECT, OR CONSEQUENTIAL DAMAGES WHATSOEVER (INCLUDING, WITHOUT LIMITATION, DAMAGES FOR LOSS OF BUSINESS PROFITS, BUSINESS INTERRUPTION, LOSS OF BUSINESS INFORMATION, OR ANY OTHER PECUNIARY LOSS) ARISING OUT OF THE USE OF OR INABILITY TO USE THE SOFTWARE PRODUCT OR THE FAILURE TO PROVIDE SUPPORT SERVICES, EVEN IF

MICROSOFT HAS BEEN ADVISED OF THE POSSIBILITY OF SUCH DAMAGES. IN ANY CASE, MICROSOFT'S ENTIRE LIABILITY UNDER ANY PROVISION OF THIS EULA SHALL BE LIMITED TO THE GREATER OF THE AMOUNT ACTUALLY PAID BY YOU FOR THE SOFTWARE PRODUCT OR U.S.$5.OO; PROVIDED, HOWEVER, IF YOU HAVE ENTERED INTO A MICROSOFT SUPPORT SERVICES AGREEMENT, MICROSOFT'S ENTIRE LIABILITY REGARDING SUPPORT SERVICES SHALL BE GOVERNED BY THE TERMS OF THAT AGREEMENT. BECAUSE SOME STATES JURISDICTIONS DO NOT ALLOW THE EXCLUSION OR LIMITATION OF LIABILITY, THE ABOVE LIMITATION MAY NOT APPLY TO YOU.